Winning Prose
&
Poetry Excerpts

Will This Circle Be Unbroken?
Grazina Smith

The line between the world I know and the unseen world around me seems very thin, as if my peripheral vision is too poor and I can't turn my head fast enough to come face-to-face with that other world. I come by this understanding naturally, descending from Lithuanian ancestors who worshiped Spirits long after most of Europe was Christian. Perkunas, the mighty Thunder God, is still acknowledged in Lithuania's public places with restaurant names, statues in parks and his ruined altars underneath our great cathedrals. It is as if the ancient religion ripples like a gentle undertow to our Christianity.

My grandmother personified the richness of that dual tradition. She was named Laima after the Goddess of Fate. She had a sixth sense and was aware of the world hovering beyond her reach...

The Fisherman Gets Home
Maureen Tolman Flannery

These days he navigates as a stranger
the contraptions of his own tackle box.
This time now he must master anew
the tricky skill of using his own reel
as the line balls up and tangles and confounds.
With infinite patience he unwinds
what his palsied fingers continue to enmesh...

Other Books by Whitney Scott

Falling in Love Again

—◆—

Love the Second Time Around

Edited & Designed
by
Whitney Scott

Outrider Press, Inc.
Crete, Illinois

Falling in Love Again is published
by Outrider Press in affiliation with
TallGrass Writers Guild.

Anastasia Bamford's "dog's journey" was
previously published in *Dogwood Girl*, 2000.

Pat Clark's "Lemon, Olives..." appeared in *Many
Mountains Moving*, summer 04/fall 05.

Sue Eisenfeld's "I Do..." was originally published
in *The Washingtonian* magazine, June 2004

Barbara Goldoeshy's "Dance Date" appeared in
The Tuesday Night Ballroom, 12-2000

Nancy Heggem's "Valentine's Day" appeared as
"Poem of Cars" in *Daily Herald*, 4-19-99

Ellaraine Lockie's "Past Prime..." was published in
Midlife Muse from Poetry Forum in 2000

Frank Matagrano's "Auditing the Heart"
appeared in *Greatest Hits*, Pudding House,
2005

Lynn Veach Sadler's "Ueo" appeared in
somewhat different form as "Bead Code" in
Sensations Magazine, 39 (Summer, 2005)

Book Design & Production
by
Whitney Scott

Outrider Press, Inc.
937 Patricia
Crete, Illinois 60417

Life is full of second chances...

Contents

2nd Place Prose

3rd Place Prose

3rd Place Poetry

1st Place Prose

Introduction

L et's face it – we all like the idea of second chances. When we lose at cards (or marbles or tennis or badminton or lawn croquet), we may find ourselves calling out, "Best two out of three," even before that final card hits on the table. The whole idea of second chances carries with it the hope of success. *Maybe this time...this time I'll get it right* we think, savoring the excitement of sweet promise.

What could be more enticing than the idea of love – euphoric, heart-quickening love – reawakened, revisited, reinvented, reaffirmed? Authors from across the nation and the world explore the tantalizing possibilities of love the second time around in our 10th anniversary edition of Outrider Press' acclaimed "Black-and-White" anthology series. Whether it's romantic attraction or the subtle interplay of flavors in a forgotten recipe, rediscovery reinvigorates as well as reinforces our sense of self, of who we are and where we've been.

I propose a toast: to the infinite variety of second chances life has to offer. Here's luck!

Whitney Scott
April, 2005

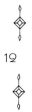

12

We Need to Speak to You
Bret Angelos

Gesso Palisade returned home to his apartment after a hard day's work. His homecoming ritual commenced immediately upon his entrance into the living room. Palisade's first and only stop in this procedure was his Lazy Boy right next to his telephone and caller ID. The red light blinked regularly and this brought joy to Palisade's eyes. The caller ID had registered 22 calls, far from the record, but fairly decent for a Tuesday. It was so good to be loved.

He didn't bother to check the phone numbers. He knew they would all follow the daily routine. Monday through Saturday between the hours of 8 A.M and 9 P.M. his sweetheart would follow the drill. Sunday was Gesso Palisade's day. That was when he got in all of his "me" time. They knew not to call on Sunday. His sweetheart was just so considerate that way.

Who was this Man-About-Town? What made him so special? Truth be told, he was a drifter. He floated from city to hamlet and to berg working temp jobs and collecting meager paychecks and no real friends. His mother was his only relation. San Diego, Tempe, Tuscaloosa, Cedar Rapids, Atlantic City, Bowling Green, and Chicago were a few of Palisade's temporary destinations. He supplemented his income by collecting high interest rate credit cards. All of his friends and sweethearts were of the corporate variety. In reality Gesso Palisade was an anarcho-capitalist. He was also a tad poco-loco.

Palisade picked up the phone and dialed up his voicemail number. Like any self-respecting loner, he took to talking to himself.

"Twenty-two missives for yours truly, Mr. Gesso Palisade. Let's see what terms of endearment slipped out of those ruby red lips of yours, my darlings."

The voicemail program kicked in and spoke to Palisade. "You have... nine new messages."

"Nine! Twenty-two calls and only nine messages! Baby, I thought we were closer than that now. Don't you trust me?"

"First message sent today at 8:17 A.M."

"We need to speak to you." A computerized female voice talked to Gesso Palisade.

All of his calls fell into one of two camps, either sexy, synthetic female voices or live, angry male voices. Palisade theorized that the angry male voices were actually the spouses or boyfriends of the sexy, synthetic female voices. These angry men wanted to confront the "other man" who so regularly stole away the affections of the fairer artificial sex. On the other hand, the women who called Gesso Palisade wanted to check in and make sure that everything was OK and that they were still on for dinner or drinks. It didn't matter that dinner or drinks never actually happened. It was the thought that counted for Gesso Palisade.

He pressed the # key and listened to the beginning of the message again.

"We need to speak to you."

"I need to speak to you too, honey."

He hit # again.

"We need to speak to you."

"Baby, I love it when you use the Royal 'We' like that. Our Queen needs to speak to us." Palisade laughed to himself as he used his own Royal lingo.

"We need to speak to you."

Palisade skipped to the next message.

"Plenty of other people need to speak to me today, sweet pea. Who's next?"

"Next message sent today at 9:47 A.M."

"Gesso, I have an important message about a private, personal business matter. Please call back at your earliest convenience."

Palisade stopped the message. He didn't like the tone in her voice.

"No small talk. No 'How's the weather? How was work? How are you feeling?' Just business this and business that. I agree the business is personal, but when you get personal, you don't have to leave it so cold. You are a true Ice Queen, my dear."

The next three messages were hang-ups.

This served to further irritate Gesso Palisade.

"You dial my number and then hang up. Hang up. Hang up. Hang up. That's pretty creepy. That's stalker material. Don't think I won't call the phone company and get them to unblock these calls. I've done it before and I'll do it again. Nobody is ever an 'anonymous' or 'unknown' caller. Everybody leaves a trail. I know I do."

Gesso Palisade moved from town to town and never left a forwarding address or phone number. This temporarily stymied his numerous creditors. But the machinery of the Credit Bureau is tireless. It relentlessly scours lending documents, tax returns, and utility bills until it gets its man. Palisade didn't care. After a couple of months in a new place he would get lonely and send all of his creditors postcards with his new contact information. The postcards would generally depict some local landmark or icon and would always include a personalized message from Gesso, complete with hugs and kisses. Gesso Palisade was just so considerate that way.

"Next message sent today at 2:53 P.M."

"Gesso Palisade. This is Mr. Anderson down at Citibank. I'm going to need you to call me today. Call Mr. Anderson at 1-800-555-4356. This call is regarding a personal business matter and it concerns Mr. Gesso Palisade."

Palisade hit pause.

"Romeo is jealous of Mr. Gesso Palisade. Hah! Juliet is mine! Star-crossed lovers, my ass! She never wanted you in the first place, Mr. Romeo Anderson. I was cool with it, though. We've got an open relationship."

"Next message sent today at 3:18 P.M."

"Gesso, I need to speak to you."

He stopped the message and savored it for a moment.

"So, so sweet, my dear. No more royal 'We'; just a simple 'I' and you used my first name. Lovely. I think I'm in love."

15

Palisade replayed the message and listened to it in its entirety.

"Gesso, I need to speak to you. This is your mother. The bank is calling me about your account again. Actually, Gesso, I've gotten calls from seven banks regarding various credit cards that you owe money on, son. I thought you told them not to call me anymore. Where did you get all of these new cards from? Call me."

Palisade's blood began to boil.

"You're calling my mother! This is intolerable."

The phone rang, but Gesso didn't answer it. The caller ID said "unavailable."

"They're unavailable. Well, so am I."

He utilized the oldest trick in the book of passive aggressive tactics. The old reliable. The silent treatment. The phone kept ringing and Palisade let the voicemail take it. He'd listen to the rest of the messages in a moment. He needed to cool off before he said or did something he might regret. His sweetheart might have made an honest mistake. Then again, seven honest mistakes didn't seem possible. It wasn't his fault that seven new brides had wed themselves in a corporate union with a deadbeat dad.

Gesso Palisade was an honest man at his core. When a bank made him a credit card offer and he signed on the dotted line, he seriously and truly believed that he would pay back any debt incurred. This belief carried over to the moments just before and just after he used said plastic purchasing power to procure some merchandise. Whether it was a new microwave, a stack of DVDs, or a trip to some exotic location, Gesso Palisade always briefly believed he would make good. This belief always evaporated when the limits were maxed out and the bills piled up.

It was a vicious cycle and Gesso loved every minute of it. The accent was on the love. With no real companionship or friends, Gesso needed his corporate lovers. They were very predictable and comfortable for Palisade. For years they would try and recover what was owed, no matter how small the amount. They'd keep calling and he'd keep playing the coy young gentleman. When they tired of the cat-and-mouse game, years would have passed, and it would be time for a whole new round of credit card offers. Gesso learned early on that no matter how bad the credit, it can never be ruined completely. Chop the arm off the octopus and it will re-grow the limb. The offers would start small, but they'd be numerous. Ten three hundred dollar cards were almost as good as one three thousand dollar card and it afforded oh so many new friends. Gesso Palisade called it anarcho-capitalism. It was Gesso's own personal version of S&M.

Palisade listened to the remaining messages. One was from another outraged husband from Household Bank and the other was from a new girl that Gesso had met from Aspire Visa. He thought about her for a moment. Man, she had a high interest rate! You look at her with that card and the first thing that catches your eye is her giant interest rate. Gesso adored credit card lovers with a little extra luggage in the trunk.

The final call was left while Gesso was pouting with the silent treatment. It was another hang up. He put the phone down and went to the fridge for a beer. It was closing in on nine at night. There wasn't much more time for casual conversation. He sat in his Lazy Boy and waited. He longed for another call. He needed to speak to somebody. He thought it might be nice to hear from Sophia. She was a nice girl from BankOne. Sophia didn't have much in the way of an interest rate, but she had personality. If only Sophia needed to speak with him. It would all be so, so lovely.

The phone rang. Gesso answered.

"Sophia? Is that you?"

A sexy, synthetic female voice answered, "We need to speak to you. Please hold for a representative. We need to speak to you. Please hold."

"Come on, Sophia. Answer me. I need to speak to you."

"Hello? Hello? Gesso? We need to speak to you. Are you there?"

"Sophia? Is that you Sophia?"

"No, this is Jennie from CapitalOne. Gesso, I need to speak to you."

"Jennie? Have we met? I'm sure we've talked."

"I don't think so, Mr. Palisade."

"A touch formal now, Jennie. I thought we were on a first-name basis."

"Mr. Palisade, I need to speak to you about your account."

"My account? Why is everything always about my account? What about your account? I thought this was a two-way relationship, Jennie. Where's the give and take? I know I've been doing most of the taking lately, but that happens sometimes. I'm the Yin to your Yang. Am I right, Jennie?"

"I don't know what you're talking about, Mr. Palisade. I've left several messages and received no response."

"How many, Jennie? I need to know how much you care."

"Our records indicate that we have left you almost 200 messages this year alone, Mr. Palisade."

"Two hundred? That's it. That's how much you care. I'll have you know that Sophia over at BankOne left me over 800 messages last year. Two hundred – that's just calling to say you love me. Now 800 – that's a personal commitment. Jennie, are you willing to commit to 800 calls?"

"This conversation is being recorded, Mr. Palisade. I don't know who you are or what your problem is, sir, but I do know that we have to get some money paid down on your account. Oh, and Mr. Palisade, we have left over 50 calls with Mrs. Palisade in Scottsdale, Arizona. So I've got a 250 commitment, but who's counting?"

Palisade was infuriated. "Let's leave my mother out of this! I told you people not to call her, and you went and called her. This is not her affair. This is about *our* affair, Jennie. It's between us, and I can see it's not going anywhere, so I bid you adieu. We're through, Jennie!"

Gesso hung up the phone.

A minute passed and the phone rang again. It was his mother.

"Mom, you couldn't have called at a better time."

"What's wrong, dear?"

"I'm having some problems with one of my lady friends. We just broke up. It was a bad break."

"Darling, it'll be OK. You always seem to meet new people easy enough. I'm sure another angel will be waiting for you around the corner in no time."

"It's just hard to think about that right now. Me and Jennie had been through so much together."

"What about Sophia? How's she doing?"

Before Gesso could answer an incoming call appeared on call waiting. It appeared as "anonymous."

"Hey, Mom, I've got another call coming through and I've got to take it. I'll call you tomorrow."

Palisade hit flash and switched over to the incoming anonymous caller. He paused and let the caller speak first.

"Hello...Gesso Palisade? Hello? This is Sophia from BankOne. Are you there, Mr. Palisade? We need to speak to you."

Gesso answered, "Sophia, how long has it been? You couldn't have called at a better time. I need to speak to you, too."

18

Jones Beach
Donald Everett Axinn

Let's sit right here, us just us, on our bed
         of scrubbed sand.
We'll talk without speaking, gaze out on
         old man Atlantic,
Watch his energy rhythmically build into waves,
         their lives constant and intense, but short.
Their commitment is like our fingers,
         each one of yours between each one of mine.
Behind us the dunes stand cool and collected,
         their hair, made of shore grass, shimmies
To smooth jazz sown into the whispers of the wind.

Remember how we used to laugh at existence and non-
         existence because we didn't know what else to do?
Now I must sit here without you. Last week
         I released your ashes on the water's edge
As we had agreed, to recycle your remains
         with the atoms of beginning and end.

Look, the sand crabs continue to create
         their unique style of hieroglyphics,
Messages sandpipers and gulls have learned
         to interpret and track over millennia.
It's dusk, isn't it, and for all the days
         that follow. I reach for your hand.
I want to touch you again, just one more time.
         One more time.

20

cedar's howl
Anastasia Bamford

oh red dog
my heart
has left the
building.

our time
too brief
flows mercurial
though my fingers
a wild ride
and then
you're drifting again
lazy spirals
in a deep pool.

i don't regret
even this pain
find me
again.

dog's journey
Anastasia Bamford

he has gone
and now returns
wearing new skin.
oh dog
where'd you find
such fine red fur –
i hardly knew you!

when last we met
you had an old coat
worn bare and ragged
and i held your head
as you shrugged it off
held my tears until
you'd made your getaway.

i'd ask where you've been
but your reply would be phrased
as a whiskered kiss and
contended sigh
nothing more or less.
well
let's just lie on the floor
as we've always done.

21

Strange Bedfellows
Harker Brautighan

You laughed so hard when you came
I thought you had lost your mind
I was spooked to see that much emotion set free
I felt exposed
My God, was I doing it...*wrong?*
Were you laughing at me?
No. No, it was pure joy
You came for eternity without spilling a drop.
You thought you were spurting all over
I thought I had squeezed madness out of you
You showed me the distinction between ejaculation and orgasm
And we shared the intimacy of first times
How strange for it to happen between
strangers
Afterwards I held you with one hand pushing you away
Not wanting your affection, running away from this random intimacy
loosed on us from my fingers and your laughing belly.
Bewildered when you embraced the closeness,
pulled me to you, kissed me, kissed me, and
thanked me with you fingers and your eyes
We've gone down such a long road together on this
one dangerous night
Can't we still be
strangers?

23

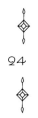

24

Gypsy Spirit
Ute Carson

The palm of my right hand stung as I swatted three mosquitoes on the splintered windowsill, leaving a trail of fresh blood streaked across the peeling white paint. The suckers had been full to bursting. With my blood! I propped my feet up on the sill with the soles pointing toward the smudged window and wryly looked at the carnage, sighing, "All dead. Like my marriages."

Nestled in the hills of Wisconsin, my cabin was only a five-minute walk from the campsite where I taught art for the summer. The sparse cabin interior of the cabin had exposed beams and buckled planks. Each time I took a step, gray dust particles flew up and tickled my nose. When my son Jack heard that I was stepping out on my own again, he gave me three oval braided throw-rugs to soften the floor. Opposite the door that always jammed stood a wrought-iron bed, a round wooden table and a rocker. My portable radio found a spot on the windowsill. I'd brought my favorite tapes, gypsy songs from Hungary.

I was ambivalent about the lone portrait of two women on the wall. Framed in ornately carved rosewood, the picture both unnerved and attracted me. The woman in front wore a cornflower-blue dress, printed with wavering wisps of white, like clouds. The fabric was tight over her broad hips and square shoulders, and her back was rigid as if stiffened in opposition. She clutched a velvet handbag parishioner-style. Over her shoulder peeked the other woman's finely-chiseled face. Tar-black strands of hair draped over her forehead like a bridal veil. Her tortoise shell earrings glittered. The rest of her body was hidden except for her hand, holding a single tiger lily – and her gracefully curved throat which seemed to pulsate slightly. The glass over the picture welled with air-bubbles like blisters on skin as if to disguise the two figures.

As the light paled, fleeting sunrays stretched across the floor like streaks of gold as the evening mist rolled in, enveloping the hills in privacy. The silence in the room slipped into my mind. I sat a long time and tried to return to that place inside myself where everything was calm. But my soul was uneasy, and an abyss of remorse was opening up. My body, like my life, was showing deep wear and tear. Even my dreams were tattered.

A month ago, with only a day's notice, I had left my third husband, Melvin. Even after he'd implored me, "Give us time – we can work it out," I had not listened. Once a certain restlessness gripped me, I was like a ship tossed high by the rising tide, my anchor torn from its moorings as I rushed toward the open sea.

Mel, who helped me raise my children from my previous marriages, was the kindest of my three mates, patient and long-suffering. This short, balding pediatrician with protruding leaf-like ears and gentle, darkly veined hands had heard the patter of tiny feet for over 30 years. Though well acquainted with poopy diapers, runny noses and bruised knees, he lacked insight into the dark recesses of grownups' souls where fears lurk and passions hide. My recurring agitation baffled him. How could he keep a hold on a centipede that scurried off at the slightest provocation?

As before, it came over me at a fancy dinner party. Suddenly the food tasted too rich and moldy odors from overstuffed furniture clogged my throat. I felt caged among the well-dressed, well-fed bodies and a single desire drove me: the need to escape. A craving for mud between my toes and the perfume of pine needles overwhelmed me. In mid-conversation I tuned out and disconnected myself from my surroundings. The lure of an unattached life drew me like bait draws a fish.

—◆—

My parents died when I was three. My grandmother raised me. In her gabled gingerbread mansion in Germany, I never lacked for physical comfort, good education or lively company. But I was short-changed on emotional nourishment.

Grandmother Ursula was like an ancient oak tree, her roots reaching deep into family soil, and her limbs and branches protecting everyone under their wide-spread umbrella. Potatoes, always still in their skins, were the staple of her diet and she served them at every meal.

"A potato is a woman's best friend. It soothes the stomach and keeps appetites grounded."

I hated potatoes even without the tough peelings. They settled in my stomach in heavy lumps.

As far back as I can remember, Grandmother Ursula tried to ground my appetites, and as I rushed excitedly from one activity to another, she sternly ordered me to sit still. "You are not a raggle-taggle gypsy, do you hear?" Her lips were pinched together like the edges of an oyster shell. She grew tall and erect whenever she reprimanded me. But she was fiercely proud of me as long as I toed the line. Grandmother Ursula tried to keep everyone together in one house, one town, and one country. "Stay with one mate, always," she warned sternly.

Her sister-in-law, my unmarried Aunt Vera, on the other hand, reminded me of that gypsy I was not supposed to be. Her long, flamboyant dresses with no pants or bras underneath swished loosely around her lanky body. She smelled of wildflowers and chamomile tea; her gold chains and wrist and anklet bangles jingled and clinked musically as she moved barefooted through her house, which was always in marvelous disarray. A child's paradise.

Every year Aunt Vera took me to a traveling circus. Once, we paid for a palm reading. The psychic cackled, "You'll roam the world, little tiger. Your spirit is restless and wild. But don't forget your camouflage, little tiger, for escape." Aunt Vera nodded approvingly.

Like warring adversaries, my rooted Grandmother Ursula and my footloose Aunt Vera fought to gain dominion over my soul.

—◇—

Wayne was an American enlisted man, strong and dashing in his uniform. He was starved for sex and I was ready for adventure. When he asked me to marry him, I said, "Let's give it a whirl."

And a whirl it was. We left Germany for the United States on a military transport. I spent most of the voyage leaning over the rocking ship's guardrail, trying to get my rebellious stomach under control, while Jack's strong heartbeat was thumping away in my womb.

Life on the army base in Georgia was dreary and monotonous. The match flame of pleasure which had attracted us soon burned low. Boredom and disappointment spread through me like poison. When Jack was two and Wayne was away on a six-week assignment, I packed our bags and, with Jack straddling my left hip, placed a note on top of the chipped fake-wood dresser that looked like all the other chipped fake-wood dressers on the base:

"I can't stay any longer. I'm becoming part of the furniture, the broken blinds and the green plastic sofa. Jack will be fine with me."

Wayne never came after us.

—◇—

We drifted across country with the wind. It was during the late sixties and we survived as members of first one commune, then another. I helped with household chores, threw pots and made macramé shawls sold at flea-markets. Eventually I also added my paintings to my sales booth.

I met Ted during a raid on our compound. The police found the usual stashes of marijuana and enough cocaine to arrest a few group members. When Ted flashed his blazing blue eyes at me, I was vulnerable. As he questioned other people, he stood very close to me and fiddled with his tie knot. His words brushed passed my ears: "You don't belong here."

He had broad hands with tapered fingers, the nails yellow and hard. But his mouth was full and smelled pleasantly of peppermint gum.

Maybe I attracted solid men. Ted was solid. He promised me that I could get rid of my Salvation Army clothes and eat fresh peaches and raspberries year round. When I told him I was pregnant, he said, "I'm gonna teach you to shoot."

He gave me a 9mm Glock, saying, "You want a weapon you can trust. You carry a weapon to protect your life. You don't want click, you want *bang.*"

But besides target practice together, there wasn't much to the relationship. The dynamics changed after we were married. Soon I felt roped like a calf at branding. Ted tried to alter my lifestyle. He grumbled about my colorful clothes, disapproved of my purple nail polish, and wanted Jack's brown curls cut.

Three months before Madeleine was born I moved out. This time I told Ted in person. He turned away from me as I spoke, his back ramrod straight.

"I saved you and your son." He shot me a look from those eyes and said, "Get lost before I lose my temper."

We bolted out the door like horses from a burning barn. Jack and I giggled, then laughed the liquid laughter of relief.

Melvin bought six of my paintings while my little son clung tightly to my legs. We could have stayed at the YMCA for a whole year on that one sale.

He was not only interested in my pictures. After carrying them gingerly, one at a time, to his car, he returned and asked, "Would you like to have dinner with me?"

"Can't you see I'm about to have a baby?"

"Well, I'm a pediatrician."

When Mel asked me to move in with him, I agreed without a moment's hesitation. I had glimpsed some unusual kindness in this small man. Jack, and later Madeleine, quickly learned to love him and knotted an umbilical cord around us all.

My firstborn and I were joined from the start. Whenever we were together, we sat on opposite ends of a couch, our bare soles flat against each other. Our mutual understanding flowed best that way.

Jack was a nature guide on rivers, and also taught survival skills to the more dedicated. When I moved into the cabin, he told me to sprinkle drops of citronella oil on my blanket and other warm hiding places to repel spiders and other insects. He lived half a day away in a cabin like mine. From there he watched for poachers and worked to preserve certain endangered species; his favorite: the Timber Rattlesnake.

—◇—

Fog had settled over the countryside. I felt snug in my cabin. While gently rocking, I noticed my breath laboring. A draft made me fetch my macramé shawl. Then I heard humming, like power lines. The wind became angry and a light rain muffled the air, spraying against the window. A shadow of change cast itself across my mood. Suddenly I smelled something like the odor given off by musty clothes. Then I spooked when a hand crawled slightly over mine like a tiny bug, and a breath slid across my shoulders like a snake. At that moment, hairpins flew into my loose hair, braiding it into a threefold cord, and pinning it to the chair.

I heard a crackling like ice splintering. Reflected in the window, I saw a zigzag line bisect the picture, and two figures stepped from the rosewood frame. Grandmother Ursula and Aunt Vera. They glided across the floor until they crowded me like two bookends. My knees knocked together.

"You are not a raggle-taggle gypsy." I knew that voice. "Go. Go," urged the other. Then the room was so still, it was ghostlike.

My heart was speeding and my mind was needle-sharp as I grabbed my bag, pulled my shawl closer and left my seductive solitude. I cut a swath through the brush and felt the wet ground beneath my bare feet. The jeep at the camp was unlocked, the keys on the driver's seat. I adjusted both mirrors and started the engine. As dawn spread its bright halo, I reached Jack's slumbering cabin, steeped in witches' smoke.

I stepped in and saw Jack dozing, his head leaning against the headboard of the bed. His right foot was bandaged and propped up on a pillow. My eyes burned as if I had stepped through a brushfire.

"Are you all right?" I nearly choked on my words.

His eyes opened slowly. "I'm all right." His irises were dilated big as pennies. He blinked and asked, "How did you know?"

"Your great-grandmother and your great-aunt returned as smoke and wind, a humming insect and a hissing snake. *They* told me."

I was so relieved that Jack was okay, I started to cry. Then I sat on his bed and listened.

"Of all snakes, the rattler bit me," he explained. "I had come upon this beautiful female. She rested on a rock, the rattle on the tip of her tail absolutely still. Her head was only an arm's length away and for a moment our eyes met. I didn't want to disturb her, so I stepped back quietly. Snakes have babies in August. I should have figured her den was near. A baby got me right above my boot."

Jack's entire face grimaced, remembering the pain. "Luckily I got only a small amount of poison. Hazards of the trade." He paused, giving me a meaningful look. "I'm so glad you're here, Mom. When I called Dad, he got here right away, disinfected the wound and gave me an shot of anti-venom."

I pulled back within my inner walls and then placed a hand on Jack's arm as if to anchor myself. "Mel is here?"

"You know snakes symbolize transformation." Jack reached for my hand and pulled it close to his chest. "Maybe this was a sign, too, like the smoke and wind and all...now go find Mel."

He was sitting on the back stoop of the cabin. Wordlessly, he patted the spot next to him for me to sit down and then looked up with his sad, longing eyes. I worked my mouth but no sounds came out.

"You don't have to run away. We can travel whenever and wherever you want." He glanced at my bare feet, muddy from my dash to the jeep. "Even with mud between your toes. Please, just...." There was little room in his steady voice for me to refuse. He sat there aglow, his face flushed with expectation. Then I saw something in Mel's eyes that I had missed before – acceptance – understanding? He would hold on to me but not hold me back.

My heart took an unexpected turn and my entire body burned hot under his glance. I dropped my defenses like a wilting flower, for I knew then that I had come home and that factions, however incompatible at times, could merge within my soul. I extended a naked foot into the dirt, drew a magic circle there and said softly, "We could try again. Gypsies never lose their wanderlust, you know. But they *do* take on fellow-travelers."

Lemon, Olives, Garlic, Oregano
Patricia Clark

A pale dusky plum color
from the vinegar brine they've
soaked in, the kalamata olives
lie now in slivers, after
the knife. In a small ramekin,
heaped, what looks like gold
pollen is the gratings of yellow zest
given up by two lemons.
Chicken pieces – breasts, thighs,
legs – mound up on a plate, plump,
ready to be browned, sprinkled
with coarse-ground kosher salt
and oregano. Tonight we journey to Greek
islands, blue seas. And the sounds
of what could be Mediterranean waves
knocking against the ferry's bow are,
instead, the waves of a Mozart concerto,
and a musician's breath knocking in, out
and around the portholes of a silver flute.
Candlelight, forks lifted, and a shiver
of wind brushing together the dark, not-
yet-ready-to-be-picked olives hanging thick
on a sun-dusted branch. Outside the glass,
it is Michigan, where snow gleams from the fat
moon, silver rolling a carpet across
the wide, wide sea of frozen grass.

32

Every Thing Counts (excerpt)
Jim Curtiss

When I wasn't examining it, I carried the ring in my pocket. I thought of it as a charm, a type of connection with my grandmother's spirit. It had been hers after all, and perhaps would bring me some of her wisdom, would see me through the turmoil of deciding between tying myself to a Central European lady or remaining Mr. Freeandeasy. Both paths beckoned, and the situation really didn't need exacerbation by the re-appearance of rock and roll hoochie-koo. But I suppose these things happen for a reason.

That February first, I told Liliana I was going into town to meet Josh. No problem, she said. She had a lot of work.

Into town I went. After two beers and no Josh, I called my messages and he'd left one saying he couldn't make it. Great.

So, being the in-love fool that I was, I hurried back to spend a quiet evening with Liliana. But when I knocked on her dorm room there was no answer.

Since I didn't have to teach the next day, I headed over to the big campus bar to see if Karel was there. Maybe we'd play some pool. Inside, I got a beer, and looked around the large hall. There were perhaps 30 square tables in the middle of the room, pool tables off to the right. Since it was a weeknight and sparsely peopled, it was easy to pick out Liliana.

She was sitting with Mr. Rock and Roll himself, Zdenek I-forget-his-last-name (OK, I *do* remember it, but I out of spite...)

Liliana was sitting with her back to me, Zdenek to her left. I could partially see his face.

Like an idiot, I skulked over to a nearby table and watched them enjoying each other's company; every now and again they'd explode in laughter.

I chugged the beer and watched, my throat burning, constricting as they carried on.

Then Liliana stood and turned in my direction. She was carrying two glasses, and as she left the table, I noticed that Zdenek was watching her. She must have felt it, too, because she spun around to bust him. He waved and smiled. When she turned forward again, she was just beaming.

The bile had never been so thick in my gut, and as Liliana came closer to my table and recognized me, she stopped short.

I stood up and nodded toward the bar. "I'll come with," I said.

When I got there, I turned and saw her trailing far behind. I ordered three beers and she came to stand beside me, placing her empties on the bar. I watched the barman fill the first glass.

"I thought you were working tonight."

"Zdenek surprised me."

Second glass.

"You seem to be having a good time."

"He's just an old friend."

Third glass.

"*Just friends* don't watch your ass as you walk away."

Silence.

I paid for the beers and picked one up. "So enjoy yourself. I'm going to my room."

"Wait. Come join us."

"Yeah, right."

As I walked around her she said, "Don't be like that."

My only comeback was too ferocious to voice, so I kept it inside and walked out the door feeling a lot shittier than when I'd gone in.

Nothing can plunge me into blackness as quickly as jealousy can, and I was neck deep in it, my breathing shallow and inadequate. I couldn't think past how happy they looked together. It was a marquee in my mind, surrounded by flashing black rock-and-roll spotlights.

It was too late to go back into the city and the pub was now out of the question, so I went for a long walk. In the middle of it, like a clever boy, I bought a pack of cigarettes at a vending machine and set about chain-smoking.

As I walked, I jumped to the conclusion that I had been given a perfect illustration of what to expect from marriage to Liliana.

I mean, hadn't I once been the other man in her life? Hadn't I caused her to end a six-year relationship?

Once a two-timer, always a two-timer.

Can't trust her.

She's sleeping with him.

Again.

After walking to exhaustion, I returned to my room. A note was stuck between the door and frame. I snatched it down but didn't read it and went inside to obsess instead.

After a fitful sleep, I got up at 7:00 and read the apologetic note from Liliana. She said she wanted to spend the night with me and could I please come and get her – anytime – when I returned from wherever I was.

I crumpled it and threw it out. I wasn't ready yet. I knew she had to teach at 8:00 and that's when I wanted to slip off campus.

I was in the shower when I heard the knock on my door – it had to be Liliana, but I didn't have anything to say.

Plus, I wanted her to feel bad as well.

St. Vitus' Cathedral opened at 9:00, and I was in a pew shortly thereafter. I needed counsel, but bad. Just 12 hours before I had been relatively sure about asking Liliana to marry me. Now I wasn't even sure I trusted her.

Shaking my head and being pissed off, I unpacked the Bible from my backpack and all I could picture was Liliana flirty and happy with Mr. Rock-and-Roll the night before.

I obsessed for a long spell until remembering where I was, and that I was actually there to cut that shit out. I closed my eyes and began to breathe deeply, berating my nasty self until I was able to drive it into the corner and back into its trunk. I shut the lid and tried to fix the latch, but again realized there wasn't one. When I opened my eyes, I looked up at the far end of the church's stained-glass windows and relaxed my shoulders, placing my hands in my lap.

My mind finally empty, I took the ring from my pocket.

It hadn't lost any of its beauty, but had somehow lost a great deal of its allure.

Marriage to an unfaithful partner was the last thing I needed. It would drive me to a number of things I'm predisposed to anyway – drink, tobacco, drugs, just to name a few. Did I really want to marry a woman who saw no problem in evenings out with old boyfriends?

I pressed the ring between my palms and closed my eyes.

I prayed for forgiveness of my sins. I prayed for Liliana and I prayed for the strength to act with integrity – to dispel my doubts and fears and to replace them with courage and integrity. I prayed for the ability to minimize the negative and maximize the positive.

Courage.

Compassion.

Patience.

I asked for help in determining whether Liliana and I belonged together. I pressed the ring harder and asked that it be blessed with the wisdom of my grandmother and the caring and love a proper marriage should possess.

When I opened my eyes again, they struggled to adjust to the sun streaming through the stained glass, and I blinked until I could see properly. I sat there, holding the ring in my hands and breathing calmly until my mind was empty.

Then I repeated my prayers.

At length I opened my eyes and appreciated the beauty of the church's architecture before I stood up. Donning my pack, I walked out, pausing only to anoint my forehead with holy water. The long, dark passage to the courtyard led me to the side exit of Prague Castle.

I felt a solemn lucidity as I walked out of the plain arched passage. There were very few people about as I exited past the cloaked castle guards and strolled across the high earthen bridge and past the gates of the closed summer garden. At the corner of the castle proper, on a whim I ducked into the touristy cafe.

36

Inside the warm seating area were five tables surrounded by walls that were painted orange. I sat down and ordered a cappuccino.

As I waited I took out the Bible, turned to the Book of James, and read. By the time the coffee came I was halfway through. I put the book down and sipped at the coffee, which burned my tongue.

Suddenly, the entrance door burst open and an older red-haired lady exploded into the room. My cup suspended in mid-air, I couldn't help but stare at her. She was wearing a long silver fox coat with a high protective collar, the wind-burned red of her cheeks and forehead evidence of the nasty weather. Her cheeks were doing a Dizzy Gillespie thing as she fought for air.

She grabbed the back of a chair and put her weight on it, breathing heavily. Looking at me as if I were an old friend, she started speaking in German and I understood nothing. I looked around to make sure she was speaking to me and when I did this, she nodded and pointed right at me.

I smiled at her, puzzled.

Behind her, a tall, grayed gentleman came in and closed the door. He was wearing a long navy blue trench coat and carrying an umbrella.

He took off his cap and came over to the red-haired lady, who continued her gestures.

The man smiled and asked if the table next to mine was free.

When I nodded, they took off their coats.

The woman spoke quickly and the man translated, "We just walked up the hill. She says I am trying to kill her."

She smiled at me and drew her finger across her throat, then gestured to her husband.

I smiled and when they started to discuss what to order, I picked up where I had been reading. I got through just two sentences before the woman started speaking to me again.

I put the book in my lap and looked up at her. The man walked around the corner to order and she continued jabbering away at me.

As I was shaking my head and shrugging my shoulders at her, the man came back to the table. He asked if I spoke German.

"Not yet," I replied.

"Ha! That's a good answer!"

The man said something to his wife that made her stop speaking to me, and I gratefully took up the book and started to read.

They spoke in German for a moment and then the man said, "Excuse me..."

Sigh. Why fight it? I closed the book and put it on the table to give them my full attention.

"Yes?"

"I'm sorry to interrupt... but my wife doesn't speak English. Do you permit me to translate for her?"

"Of course."

The woman spoke for awhile, then the man asked me how to get to the castle's National Art Gallery. I gave him the directions and he translated for her.

Then he asked me if I were a tourist. I told him I lived in Prague, and he seemed very pleased by this.

"When I was a young man," he said, "I also lived in Prague..."

The woman reached over, patted my forearm and rolled her eyes.

"... and I had the nicest Czech girl. The Czech girls are beautiful, aren't they?"

"They are."

"We were going to get married but I was in love with another girl, a German girl, and I went back to her."

"Really? Is this...?"

"No. This is my second wife."

The lady spoke while looking at me, then gestured to her husband, indicating that he would translate.

"Uh... she wants me to ask the name of your Czech girlfriend."

How did she know I had a girl? I looked at her and said, "Liliana."

"Wunderschöne name," she said.

The man asked to see a picture of Liliana, and I dug around for the snapshot we'd made in a photo booth.

He looked at it, nodding a long time before passing it over to his wife.

She nodded vigorously and said, "She is beautiful!"

I looked at the picture after she handed it back and nodded. "She is."

The man took off his glasses and leaned close to me.

"You must not lose her," he said.

I blinked at him. "Pardon?"

"Do not lose her," he emphasized.

I looked at his wife, who broke out her English again. "God is with you."

I looked at the man for clarification, but the lady patted my arm to get my attention again. "God is with you," she repeated.

Blank expression. Nodding dumbly. God was with me. It doesn't get any clearer than that.

I probably should have been overjoyed and celebratory, but the whole thing was just too direct, too crazy strange for me to handle gracefully. I thanked them and excused myself, saying it was time for me to go. I stood up and they nodded, smiling indulgently.

I wanted to ask how they knew I had a girl. How they knew I was in a crucial stage. Most of all, I wanted to ask how they knew God was with me. But I was just too weirded-out.

As I bundled up, I offered my hand to the man. He shook it and smiled. "Remember," he said.

"I will." I turned to the lady then, and as we shook she patted me on the cheek and gave me a little cherubic smile. I backed off and went around the corner to pay the waitress. On a whim, I paid for their drinks too, and walked out of the café knowing something intriguing had just happened.

—◈—

Was God really reaching out to me through those people, telling me to marry Liliana? Does it really work that way?

You can call it bullshit all you want – all I know is that I prayed earnestly and believingly, and I got what I asked for.

At least, that's how I interpreted it, and on my way home after meeting the "Germans," I convinced myself that I had to forgive Liliana for her meeting with rock-and-roll boy the night before. But I also had to be sure she had such things out of her system.

I went straight back to her room and knocked, halfway wanting *him* to answer the door so I could simply turn my back on the task laid before me.

But no. She was there, alone.

Her puffy eyes turned *on* when she saw me and she hugged me so hard I stumbled backwards.

It was a nice re-affirmation about the state of us, and when she said, "I'm so sorry! I didn't sleep at all last night," I knew everything would be fine.

40

Shawangunk Mountain Love

Joanne Dalbo

I didn't fall in love with you at first,
Impressed though by your hard and sculpted forms
And how the waters from your hewn stone burst,
Into a shimmering pool where you were born.

Inside my head was I as I jogged by,
A glance at most at your cloak hemlock green.
Your breath on my cheek I caught on the fly,
Your soft sigh smelling sweet warm piney clean.

It took three times or more before I felt
That tingle when I stood inside your space,
And five times more before my heart would melt
When you drew me into your warm embrace.

As you became familiar to me
Time grew a love at first I could not see.

42

The Cooking Lesson
Marcy Darin

S he had said yes. How could she refuse? She was a 50-year-old
divorcee with three kids at home and no man's phone number
saved on her cell. He was a 37-year-old Italian artist who found
her attractive enough to ask to the movies.

It was heady stuff, snagging a date with a man 13 years her junior.
Especially a man who spoke another language and had never been
inside a Walmart.

His business card, left on the kitchen counter overnight, was
splattered with her morning coffee, thanks to that irritating leaky
spout. This was something else that aggravated her about her ex-
husband, besides the fact that he was gay and never bothered to
mention this detail before the wedding.

The three children she had conceived were the tender gifts she
took from this ill-fated union. Miracles, really. All of them. As a 20-
year-old French major, she had adored Albert Camus, the existentialist
who had advised to "live to the point of tears." This had not been
difficult for her, although she was sure this was not what Camus had
in mind. In the early years, her sexual overtures to her husband had
been repudiated, first gently, then with the rage of a man living a lie.
She had been so busy changing diapers, wiping noses and making play
dough she hardly noticed she didn't have a marriage. She and her kids
had been window dressing, the appropriate "accoutrements" for a man
of her husband's station. When he refused to do what any husband
might have done willingly – driven a baby with pneumonia to the
emergency room, gone to a daughter's school play, held her hand as
she awaited the results of a biopsy – she had been shell-shocked by
his cruelty.

When a therapist pointedly asked her how long would she
subject her kids to her husband's abuse, her throat tightened until
she felt like vomiting. After 18 years, she left him, scraping money from
three jobs to pay a lawyer.

That was five years ago. Considering how things might have turned out, life was pretty good. True to his narcissistic nature, her ex-husband moved to a lakefront studio...Impossibly small for three almost teen-agers, but perfect for her weekend stays. Twice each month, she packed up and switched to her ex's. How she hated that word, but there didn't seem to be a more suitable one for the moment. The kids stayed put, free to play in a basketball league, babysit, or simply wrestle each other until the downstairs neighbor thumped his broom on the ceiling. Sometimes the hardest part was deciding which books to take.

It was a delicious decision. Faced with the delight of nights uncomplicated by doing laundry, helping to unravel the mysteries of fractions, or nagging about whose turn for dishes, she contemplated her reading selections with care.

True, this was her ex-husband's apartment overlooking Belmont Harbor. Yet every other weekend, it was transformed into a bachelorette pad, a safe place to launch her adventures in the city. Just two weeks ago, she had led a 50-year-old investment advisor, her sole Internet conquest, to the lakeside apartment seven floors above Lake Michigan.

He turned out to be obsessive-compulsive in an uncharming way. Hours after eating, his placemat was still on his table, free of crumbs, wrinkles or other disabling things. Those crystal vases on the faux fireplace had four gladiolas apiece. When she had told him she loved being kissed by him, he responded with a cool, "Likewise."

Paolo was different; expressive to the degree that the obsessive guy had not been. She had asked him, or had he invited himself? She had felt emboldened by the fact that he was leaving for Milan the next day, taking with him any embarrassment or memory of the evening.

His eyes were deep and brown and sad. The tenant in her sister's basement apartment for four months, he'd been invited by their mutual friend to exhibit his work in America. Unlike her sister, who still winced at Paolo's art – multi-textured prints arguing for "Less War, More Viagra" – she was careful to stop in front of every montage, struggling to say something brilliant and insightful during the times she'd exchanged a few words with him at her sister's place. Most of his work featured photographs of pretty women with bold red text streaming across their flattened tummies. He said that his work was a commentary on the consumer culture that dominated MTV. And then one Sunday afternoon when she was bushwhacking through Morton Arboretum, he had phoned her on her cell. Immediately, she imagined her sister crushed by a runaway Pepsi truck. Why else would this stranger call?

Now on this particular afternoon, she had shaved her legs and dressed more carefully than usual. Black was always a good choice, sexy and slimming. Turquoise earrings dangled just shy of her turtleneck's top. She decided on jeans, which snapped across her padded abdomen without too much complaint.

Lately she had been rubbing her own feet at night with peppermint cream. She remembered reading once how women who had been raped could be healed by massage, coaxed into health by a gentle hand. It was like that for her now. After leaving her ex-husband, she had been haunted, jumping back when a man came too close to her. Funny, she thought, how change is almost imperceptible. You can turn a corner and not even know it until you're blocks ahead.

Last year, the sight of fathers with toddler sons in the sandbox, excited daughters pedaling new bikes while their winded fathers kept pace on foot – all these scenes had made her cry. It had never been that way for her kids. Now she could watch families in the tot lots and be happy for them.

45

And for her own kids. She was so proud of herself, supporting her family through her writing. It was hard work, and she took extra assignments to make her paycheck stretch. But life was so much more peaceful. They could breathe.

Meanwhile, she had carved out this afternoon, and the night that followed for herself.

Paolo hadn't been in the Midwest long enough to develop a taste for soda pop, so had asked for water. She went to the Seven Seas Store on Broadway, choosing her purchases carefully. She bought spring water, a small bottle of Seltzer, and some pretzels. She put the snacks in a blue bowl and the water to chill in the f ridge. And waited. When the buzzer sounded, she almost jumped out of her skin.

The Parking Angel had been with them. (A friend swore by these practical cherubs who were replacing St. Christopher as patrons of travel, at least city travel).

She and Paolo had found a spot allowing them to tackle the six blocks to the theater on foot. Though he spoke in broken English, they managed to discuss the state of welfare reform in the US and Italy and the role of the Communist Party. She imagined that people were staring at her, other women over 50 nodding a silent, "You go, girl," A guy, an Italian guy who likes to cook...

He bought her popcorn when she explained that she was incapable of watching a movie without the salty taste of popcorn in her mouth. In Italy, he said, you had ice cream at movies. She was pleased with herself.... Here she was next to a real, honest to goodness Italian, watching a movie in Spanish with English subtitles. Like she was the heroine of a Fellini flick. The simple act of plunking your $10 bill down and reading the subtitles became an exotic plunge into a foreign country.

At her suggestion, they had seen the *Motorcycle Diaries*, a celluloid account of a young Che Guevara's road trip across South America. One scene stuck in her mind: His swimming the Amazon to reach the patients in a leper colony. Gulf between patients and doctors...the Amazon and their tears. Paolo explained that Che, less known in America, was an icon in Italy.

On the way back, they stopped at Dominick's to shop for dinner. She carried the basket while he picked out the groceries. This, too, was a first, being with a male who actually shopped. Oh, she had seen them with cellphones to their ears, getting long distance advice on what cereal to buy and *the just get whatever is on sale*. But never had she accompanied a living, breathing male to a supermarket checkout. Two bottles of Chardonnay lay in the basket. Her heart skipped a beat when she felt the weight of the bottles, pondering their meaning.

Waiting in the checkout, her mind recalled a time 30 thirty years ago when she took a bus from her Michigan college to rendezvous with an older man (in his 30s) she'd met working summers as a cashier at a convenience store. He had cooked for her, too: Steaks, with a guitar serenade of John Denver songs. And he had taught her the rudiments of lovemaking, an X-rated professor Henry Higgins with a willing Eliza.

─◈─

Now she and Paolo made their way back quickly to the lakeside apartment, each carrying an offering for the feast. Nervously, she freed the wine bottles from their brown bag prison, placing one on the counter and the other in the fridge.

"The secret of the Italian kitchen is simplicity," he whispered. She sipped her wine while he chopped several pearly white cloves of garlic. Soon these were floating in a pond of olive oil. She loved watching him; secretly, nothing made her happier than someone cooking for her, especially a dark Italian with soulful eyes that looked like they were crying even when they weren't.

She pulled up a stool and balanced herself, nervously flicking the translucent peels of garlic from the counter, their dinner table. The salmon flaked willingly under the gentle pressure of her fork.

Oh, if her friends could see her now, woman of the world. Turning from the stove, he came toward her, filling their glasses. And clinking a toast.

They talked about his childhood, the rigidity of the Italian educational system, the idiocy of the Iraq war. Both his parents were artists. His mother worked for an advertising agency. This was new, he said, Italian mothers working outside the home.

The fruity wine and animated conversation had left her woozy. She was now an interloper in his world, drifting between sips of wine and a breathy promise. "I will come see you when I return to America..." He reached for her, placing a bristly kiss on her lips. They drifted to the couch, an uncomfortable futon folded in an upright position. He pulled her to his side while lowering the futon's back

Yielding to his gentle pressure, she had leaned back onto a Chinese silk pillow. Her hands gripped his as he tugged at her sweater. He touched her breasts, "Beautiful," he whispered. "You are so beautiful." Behind them, the traffic of Lake Shore Drive droned on. Behind the traffic was a great lake reflecting gauzy harbor lights. It made her feel a possibility that even a woman long ignored could feel desirable once more.

She vaguely remembered reading a quote about Henry James observing that kindness, kindness and kindness were the three most important qualities. After five years of celibacy, she was ready to open herself to a man, this man. The steel grey years of being alone, of raising three kids on her own, were melting into this sweet embrace. Her daughter's suicide attempt, (explained, in part, she thought, by her ex-husband's pathological selfishness), the monthly roulette of bill paying, the scrounging for spare change in drawers and taking it to the machine at Jewel for redemption – could this be assuaged by a lover's embrace?

She imagined this painting of Michelangelo's, the one where God is reaching over to touch the outstretched hand of Adam. In that space hung the universal mystery; in the eventual touch, transcendence. She and Paolo were suspended there now.

He said he had a condom. Yes? No? Yes? As tempting as it was, she did not want to make love with this charming stranger. She would wait, wait for someone she knew better, someone who knew her love of Milky Ways and pink roses.

He left at midnight, refusing her offers of dark coffee. Alone, she touched her chin; it felt itchy from his not-so-soft beard. The next evening, she would tell her kids she had tripped on an old rug, suffering a carpet burn. Yeah, they would say. Mom as habitual klutz. Recovering her mothering instincts, she reluctantly covered her bare skin with antibiotic cream and a Band-Aid. Every now and then, she would touch it and smile. The next day, she would buy more garlic.

48

Fire Flies
Catherine Denby

Her first love was dead. So was her second, and she was only sixteen. But the dead poets held her like none of the boys in town.

Night darkened the sea into a black sheet wave-scrawled with white lines, immersing her in a negative page of poetry. Amanda walked out of the water. Slipping on a short, white terrycloth robe, she fished a small jar from its pocket and reexamined the moth with orange and black wings, bold as any butterfly's. Pocketing it, she picked up a large jar filled mostly with moths and, cocking her butterfly net over her shoulder, hiked off into the dunes. She'd found one amazing specimen. One wasn't enough; she had to find another. There had to be two.

Amanda, seeking solitude, had taken up bug collecting with a vengeance. She already had twice the number of specimens required for her upcoming junior year Biology project, but the net slung over her shoulder offered an excuse for spending her days alone, roaming the dunes.

Amanda wove through dark, wavy lines of sea grass, singing Poe's lines to herself. "It was many and many a year ago in a kingdom by the sea, Amanda there lived..."

She stopped, Poe's poetry swallowed in heart-stopping-but-still-beating terror. For it was still beating. Not still, wildly now, and she could hear it, just the other side of the dune. She fell to her belly, moving up the sliding flank of sand like her little brother's lizard.

If her body was a lizard's, her heart was not her own, either. Her heart was a supple drum of skin, a loud drumming of skin on skin. For, lifting her head above the dune's crest, she saw him and her heart was in his hands.

A satyr, that was her first impression: a glint-eyed, goat-legged satyr with a goatee.. But on closer inspection, she saw the heavily furred thighs were baggy pants bunched up round bone-y, bare legs wrapped round a joined pair of drums. He was thin and wiry, all manic movement, and so pale he seemed to shine, all white in the moonlight, except for the dark curling triangle of hair on his bare chest and a wild whorl of dark hair on his head.

49

Flinging back his head, he began singing, chanting, shouting out at break-neck speed, drumming a wild dance for words that were like broken glass, sharp with sorrow, but shining so sharply they cut through, they cut through it all. Words that leapt out at her, leapt into the air because they were a dance on broken glass. Words that howled with human pain and the pure pleasure of a wolf: giving voice to the night, white teeth to the stars.

Her fear suddenly as outmoded as crawling, she stood and moved down the dune toward him. He too was under the spell of the hypnotic, narcotic words, and didn't register her until she was standing in front of him.

"...Who bared their brains to Heaven under the El and saw Mohammedan angels staggering on tenement roofs illuminate, who..." He broke off. Saw. Saw her standing there, all wet. Water beading her breasts; the tan line, breaking white, right at the sandy edge of her suit. And wanted to plunge into her like an ocean.

"Whooee!" he said softly, staring at her. "So it's not 'the men in the white coats' or 'the men with the butterfly nets' coming to take me away – it's a woman!"

Amanda stared back at him, abashed. She'd never been called that before, a woman.

"Was that your poem?" she asked, awed.

"*Howl?*" he laughed, no, howled. "If I were a wolf on the prowl, out to fleece the furry white lamb..." he ran a finger lightly down the edge of her open robe, skirting skin, "that'd be the perfect line. Perfect lines! Ginsberg! Allen Ginsberg, greatest poet alive!"

"T.S. Eliot," Amanda countered.

"I'm talking about *alive*. Eliot...I think the guy's shell-shocked, a shell! 'We are the hollow men.' Well if I am, I'm bongos! Bonkers! We are the howlin' men!" he cried, his face pure glee gleaming in the moonlight.

They stared at each other. Amanda, feeling awkward, began, "You're from..."

"Greenwich Village. I go to the New School there. Be a junior next year, a film major. But Mona, my mother, she moves here! From The Village to this village!"

He swung round to survey the town's white cupolas and towers, cresting like foam behind the pale wave of the dune.

"You got some crazy architecture! I'm thinking man – 'Ozymandias and his pleasure domes' – but the place is totally square. *Ozzie and Harriet.*"

He surveyed her body, admiring her build.

"But you, you're certainly not square." His eyes wandering to her breasts, he murmured, "'Ozymandias and his pleasure domes.' How old did you say you were?"

"Oh I'll be a junior, too," Amanda said quickly.

"Home for the summer, huh? I'm going back tomorrow. Where do you go to – "

"Oh look! The fireflies are out! They – "

"A Biology Major, eh? Do you – "

Bent on distracting him, Amanda showed him the large bug jar she'd been carrying, saying," Look at that! That's a dragonfly. And the little one that looks kinda like it, that's a damsel fly. They're hard to catch 'cause they're so fast."

"The damsel and the dragon. The damsel now, she needs a prince to rescue her." Appointing himself to the task, he began unscrewing the cap. Amanda grabbed back the jar.

"He's the frog that eats them both. Beauty in the Beast."

"You're an English major, aren't you?"

"And the wasps! They – "

"Yeah, this is a real WASP town, isn't it?"

"You sound like my dad. I wrote him this poem..." She stopped, flustered.

"A poetess. Let's hear it!."

"A poet," she corrected curtly, but began mumbling, "I don't know, it's not very good..."

"I dare you."

Taking a deep breath, Amanda plunged into the poem, reciting swiftly, in monotone, "Wasps are poets, riding the wind, wind writers, building paper palaces they – I can't!" She broke off, glaring at him.

"But that's beautiful! Go on."

"Oh the beautiful stuff," she burst out miserably. "The beautiful stuff's too hard to say!" She fished the little jar out of her robe and offered it to him instead.

"Here – now here's a real beauty! An orange moth. I was sitting on some driftwood, watching the sun set, and it just sets down beside me on..."

He interrupted her, re-saying her words "The sun set, set down beside me..."

"On a...on a stalk of dune grass..."

"Grass stalked by the sun..."

"That's what I thought! Well, sorta. Usually moths, they go for the fire. But this moth, orange and black and all, it was! It *was* the fire."

"...She's stalking the sun, then the sun's talking back, in orange and black – "

"In tongues of fire!" she finished triumphantly.

"A poet's tongue," he said.

"You've never been kissed...like that," he said slowly, carefully.

"Nope!" Amanda admitted merrily.

"What! What? How old are you?"

"I'm...16," Amanda admitted reluctantly, glad at least her last birthday was past, "and I definitely don't want to be 'sweet' 16," she added fiercely.

"Sixteen! You're jailbait! You...I'd better split," he said, backing away.

He turned, bending to pick up his bongos. And she did it, the first really crazy thing she'd ever done in her life – she snatched up the butterfly net and netted his head. Then let go, laughing. He turned and stared at her through the white netting.

Giggling, she sang off key, "Here comes the bride."

"Hey, I'm a filmmaker; I travel light, like film over light; don't wanna become no solid citizen, get married, get mortgaged."

He looked back at the town crowning the dunes.

"Last night in Nowheresville, and you come out of nowhere," he murmured. Then smiled slowly, tracking the net's white lines, thinking maybe he could stay on the road and stay with her, following the white lines while she, the rider/writer, followed the black lines, stopping at the signs, yielding to the symbols. The yellow flashing symbols, he thought, eyes full of fireflies.

"You," he said appreciatively, "you're fucking crazy."

"Well, since I'm 'fucking,' what's a little kiss," she asked boldly, but blushed.

Shaking his head, removing the netting, he said cautiously, "I guess we can see what develops." Joking again, gesturing to the surrounding night, he added, "We've got this darkroom to ourselves."

Striking a pose, Amanda said in her best Mae West voice, "I'm already developed!"

"What...what'd you say your name was?"

"You said Ginsberg. But – "

"OK... Phil Rhea! But my friends call me names. X ray, X-rated, Film/man. Director, producer and cameraman of a short film in negative called *In Negative Harlem*. And you?"

"Amanda Lynn McCloud. A...a poet."

"A mandolin – isn't that a kind of lute or lyre?" In catching this pun, he captured her heart.

She laughed. "Yeah. A poet, pickin' the lute for the song, pickin' the loot for the jewels, or...well, a poet's a kind of liar, right?"

"Better than a 'bullshit artist,' I guess. More *poetic*."

Fingering the net, he continued softly, "You catch something with all those lines, and it's alive. But then, then it becomes something you can pin down, something you can label."

He looked up, challenge writ in his eyes. Amanda stiffened, for the first time hearing poetry poetically debunked, but rose to the occasion. A line came to mind, like all her best lines came to her – like damsel flies, like dragonflies – coming of the blue.

"A poet lays his...*her*...life on the line," she declared, as if stating the distillation of long thinking instead of something she just thought up.

"You're something else. Hey, I thought at first, a mermaid maybe. But your tale isn't your body, is it? It's stranger than that, though, God knows, it's lured me into deep waters already...Sirens, sirens that sing you off course. For a single guy, On the Road, one woman..."

His voice fell ominously, but he was staring at her, she thought, like a moth ready to throw himself into the fire.

"Then have 'one for the road,'" she offered.

That did it; cracked him up. "One for the road! Hey, man, where'd you learn to talk like that?"

"It's something my dad always says," Amanda said, reduced to mumbling again.

"Well, daddy-o must know...Yeah, man, maybe a mermaid, but look at you with all your wings." He waved at her bug jars and at the fireflies winking conspiratorially all around them. "Baby, you got me flying!" he cried, and grabbed her.

She stiffened, shivering in the summer air.

"Hey, don't be scared. I'm not playing with you, I'm playing *with* you. Playing with words, for play...foreplay," he growled and, turning, caught a firefly and held it up for her inspection.

"Look, it starts out that things look black. But in the end the body says, 'There's light...there's light in the body, too!'"

"God bugs with lights in their butts," Amanda blurted out, then stopped, embarrassed.

"I'm...bare-assed again, huh?" he teased, and then leaped from biology straight into theology. "So God butts in. But God must be...well strange. A strange God, that's the only God I'll have before me! If there's a God in whose image I'm made, well, he's crazy man, crazy! God," he tapped his head, "is bigger than we think. So don't *think* you're crazy, Baby, *be it*."

He waved the winking firefly in her face.

He took the bug and zigzagged its lit, living end down his arm, leaving a neon lightning streak, confiding, "I'm making a film about Prometheus. He takes delight! Heavenly delight! And the American eagles are tearing him apart."

Torn between disgust and elation, Amanda watched him snatch another out of the air and streak its glow-in-the-dark guts over the exposed skin of her own arm. It was like becoming blood brothers, she thought queasily. This gory bug squashing, for a shared vein of light.

"I'll kill for the perfect image," he said harshly. "I'll turn on life, to turn on the light!"

He cupped another out of the air, and stubbed it against her cheek, dragging it down her neck to the swell of her breast, stopping at the top of her swimsuit. They stared at each other, and then in one fluid motion he stripped off her terrycloth robe.

Amanda ran. Left him standing there, looking stranded in the sand, clutching her robe like a white flag. She wheeled, caught a firefly. Eyes locked with his, she deliberately smooshed it against her lips: cake-y, neon lipstick. Then dribbled it down her chin and neck, and down to her other breast.

Grabbing up the bug jar, Phil opened it and scooped out a fistful of fluttering white moths. He dropped the jar, then dropped his pants. Shocking the shock right out of her, he smeared the living, dying moths all over himself, until he was a powdery white in the night. Catching and dispatching more fireflies, he scrawled them all over his shiny, Halloween-y skin until it swarmed with sulfur-y symbols, illuminated letters. Iridescent, phosphorescent, he moved toward her, his hand crammed with another fistful of floury moths. Apparitional as an Aztec priest with a handful of still beating heart, he began smashing pulpy, palpitating bodies against her skin, stripping off her suit and repainting her paleness with this stranger whiteness. Then he began methodically mapping her with glowing swirls, spirals and comet tails made of trailed fireflies.

They stared at each other's strange new skins. Repulsive and radiant. Barbaric...beautiful and beastly, both. A gory glory. Phil stepped back, grinning ghoulishly.

54

"Ah, my lady, did you know moths can't fly without the dust on their wings? But with this neon green on, this moon dust moth dust...we're gonna fly, you and I, we're gonna fly!"

He began dancing around in the sand, yelling, "We're human hieroglyphics! We can read ourselves into everything! We can make the darkness dance and sing down the sky!"

Released, electrified, Amanda leaped after him, light streaking naked in the night. They were whirling dervishes, dancing in the sand, bodies turned into dust that flew. Incandescent, fluorescent, they were moonlit, sunstreaked creatures. Loony, sunstroked, mad. Live wires, glowing with a green-y light. Wired messages, speeding through the night: signaling a brand new discovery of fire. The branded body, the signaling skin.

"We glow in the dark, "Amanda gasped, "like uranium!"

"You're radiant!"

"Irradiated!" she shouted, whirling round him

"We're radioactive, live! We're the split atom, and..." He grabbed her to him, "Reunited! We're Adam and Eve!"

Leaving Paris
Randall DeVallance

The ball was thrown high, high enough that the play-by-play man felt the need to comment on it, as he did every time DeMolay served. When it reached the apex of its flight, it hung for a moment – inertia and gravity, in their tug of war, having reached a standstill – a neon-yellow blemish against the faces of a thousand tiered tennis enthusiasts who gasped their appreciation in a collective "Ah!" When gravity, inevitably, gained the upper hand, the ball began its spiraling descent, hurtling towards the man known as 'Jacque the Rock' to his most fervent supporters. Like a seasoned limbo champion, he arched his back, shoulders parallel with the ground, and held his racket perpendicular to his side; his arm, fully extended, showed sinewy muscles that rippled with anticipation. Eyes directed towards the heavens, he traced the ball's tragic fall, from the airy heights of Roland Garros to the steaming clay beneath his customized K-Swiss.

And then...a crack! As though it were spring-loaded, DeMolay's body erupted into motion, a furious windmill; swinging his racket high, he struck the fuzzy orb cleanly on its face and launched it with laser-like velocity at his adversary, who stood rooted in place like a shell-shocked weed.

"Net," said the line judge.

DeMolay watched the ball pitter-pattering at the foot of the nylon at mid-court. It was his seventh double-fault.

"You suck!" yelled someone from the upper deck.

"Quiet, please," said the line judge.

DeMolay finished out the match, a crushing loss to virtual unknown Spencer Shoe, ranked 137th in the world. Even worse than the humiliation of losing to a Yank amateur on French soil was the headline that greeted him the following morning as he sat down for his customary breakfast of toast and orange juice: "DeMolay Has Seen His Day." To be dismissed in rhyme, he felt, was the height of ignominy.

These feelings were compounded when he received a tearful phone call from his girlfriend, Tamara. Her distress could also be traced to the news wires, this time her hometown paper, the *Pittsburgh Post-Gazette*: "Shoe Stomps the Competition," it read, accompanied by an Op/Ed piece entitled, most bewilderingly, "For DeMolay, the Shoe is on the Other Foot."

"What does that mean?" asked Jacque.

"It means you're washed-up," said Tamara, who, being American, had a succinct and often jarring way of delivering the truth. "You're a terrible tennis player," she added.

"I see."

"No, you don't see," she snapped. Jacque marveled at Tamara's ability to transcend her grief. "If you did see, you would have given up the sport a long time ago."

"But I love playing tennis..."

"Oh, can it! You don't love tennis. You mope every time a tournament comes along. You barely even practice anymore. You're getting old, Jacque..."

"I'm only 32."

"That's old for a tennis player."

"What about the money?" he asked.

"That was fine, back when you could actually win a match. You'd probably make more now managing a grocery store."

"Well, thanks for cheering me up."

"You want cheering up? Buy yourself a Hallmark card. But don't ask me to keep excusing you for letting your life go to shit."

Jacque was racking his brain for an exceptionally biting comeback when he heard the line go dead. Tamara had an exquisite sense of timing, especially when it came to arguments. Manipulation and subjugation, he thought, those were Tamara's true talents. She would have made an excellent psychologist.

DeMolay got dressed and left his room at the Saint Germain Holiday Inn. His lodgings had been a last-minute choice, borne of necessity after his coach, Bertrand, had informed him that his sole remaining sponsor, Texas-based Riggings Athletic Gear, had refused to put up the funds for a two-week stay at the Hotel Bel Ami. The Saint Germain Holiday Inn had the advantage of familiarity; it was like any other Holiday Inn anywhere in the world, albeit slightly 'Frenchified' – a few gaudy, ornamental touches on an otherwise slipshod design. This concept was perhaps best encapsulated by the lid of DeMolay's toilet, an Italian marble piece with gold inlay, which, when lifted, revealed a cracked, plastic bowl conspicuously absent of water. The latter was due to a broken pipe, which management had assured would be fixed as soon as possible – "as soon as possible," apparently, being sometime after seven days, which is how long DeMolay had been relegated to using the lobby restroom to relieve himself. His subsequent calls to the desk had been received with a sigh worthy of Marie Antoinette; "You've got your marble toilet lid," it seemed to say, "What the hell else do you want?"

The hallways of the Saint Germain Holiday Inn were not only narrow, but long to the point of absurdity, so that the walls, rather than run parallel, seemed to angle slowly toward one another, terminating at a sharp point somewhere far in the distance. This trick of perspective, coupled with the serpentine patterns of the floor carpet, set DeMolay's mind reeling, and his thoughts fell inevitably on Tamara: Tamara, at home in Pittsburgh; Tamara, driving to and from the bank; Tamara, stopping by Saint Ann's to pick up their daughter, Marguerite; Tamara, cooking dinner; Tamara, washing clothes; Tamara doing the dishes. There was something steadfastly American in the way Tamara trudged through life, never slowing down, never questioning. It was this undying conviction, and the stability it provided, that Jacque found her most admirable quality, and yet, it never failed to send a chill through him when he considered it for too long.

Leaving through the Gothic double doors (another superfluous amenity) at the front of the lobby, Jacque stepped out onto Rue Cavalier, into the heat and haze of Norman summer. He chose a direction, left, and started walking, sometimes up and sometimes down, as the uneven concrete demanded. He passed a café on his left, a smattering of umbrella-shielded tables spread across the sidewalk, where old men swirled their wine glasses and young, brooding couples frowned over their café crèmes; farther up to his right, a string of boutiques had attracted a herd of glamorous waifs, long-limbed beauties who eyed the dresses and bags displayed in the windows with detached amusement. Watching the leisurely pace of Saint Germain, the people drifting and bobbing like buoys in a dead sea, DeMolay realized that, after a decade spent living there, America had become a part of him, too. His motherland he viewed now through a foreigner's eyes, and what he saw was movement, movement without focus, without end point or destination. No goal existed; it was the movement of the restless, the pacing of one stuck in an empty room. He thought about this as he passed the fountain on Rue Amélie, the spot where, 12 years earlier, he'd held a young, American exchange student named Tamara Banks in his arms and kissed her for the first time. How decrepit it looked now, the marble cracked, covered in creeper vines and stained with mildew. The water had all but dried up; the spigots had been turned off and the bowl held only a few stagnant puddles choked with leaves. The city had not seen rain in over a month and a half. Paris was in a drought.

When he had finished his walk, DeMolay packed his bags and called for a taxi to take him to the airport. He had succeeded in upgrading his ticket, snagging a seat on the redeye to New York after another passenger had cancelled last minute. His family would not be expecting him for at least another three days. Jacque felt the surprise might do them good. He thought of Marguerite's expression as he walked through the door, how happy she would be to see him. The name "Marguerite" had been Tamara's idea, pretty girls' names being "one thing the French got right." Jacque realized he had forgotten to buy his daughter a present, and he used the hours before his departure searching the meager offerings of Charles de Gaulle International, settling finally on a souvenir pen and a stack of notebooks for her to write her stories in. Marguerite, he was proud to tell people, had a certain knack for writing. She had a knack for almost everything she tried: painting, sculpting, poetry, music, sports. There was a vigor with which she attacked life, a tiny sponge trying to soak up everything at once; he wasn't sure if it was the normal exuberance of an eight-year-old or something intrinsic to her personality, but he hoped she would never lose that fire, would never stop finding joy in discovery.

The flight itself was without event, a lack of turbulence making for a serene passage, as if the plane were gliding on a surface of ice. Unable to sleep, DeMolay browsed through a magazine he had purchased at an airport newsstand. The cover had caught his eye, specifically one of the smaller headlines near the bottom-left of the page, promising analysis and dissection of "The Ten Greatest Tennis Matches of the Nineties." Jacque was astounded to see his photograph underneath, taken 12 years ago at the final of the NEC Open in Phoenix. Tagged by *The Sporting News* as "one to watch," the 20-year-old DeMolay had upset Pete Sampras in a five-set marathon the press had dubbed, as befit the times, "Desert Storm II." DeMolay read the article, a set-by-set breakdown of the entire match, and as the words touched his eyes and coursed deep into the recesses of his brain, the memories unfolded, stretched themselves out like an old, forgotten reel of film removed from its canister, so that he could almost feel the Arizona sun beating down on his neck and the blisters that tore at his feet as he navigated the baseline. Those were the days of infinite promise, the days when things came easy, when tennis and love and life had been a source of constant joy. Which, as he arrived at the final period of the final sentence, made the return to his present reality that much harder to comprehend.

Touching down at LaGuardia just before dawn, it was onto a Greyhound for the seven-hour drive to Pittsburgh. Jacque watched the familiar scenery roll by, fields interspersed with trees, followed by hills and the occasional farmhouse, the sort of dour landscape destined to be enshrined on the walls of a local McDonald's. He fought down a sudden craving for French fries and dozed the majority of the trip, preferring his dreams to the gray reality of Pennsylvania's skies.

It was early evening when they arrived in Pittsburgh. Sitting in the back of a Yellow Cab, winding through the East End toward his home in Point Breeze, Jacque imagined the reception he was about to receive. Marguerite would run to him, no doubt, clutching a picture or story or whatever it was she was working on in school. He would look at it, smile, and tell her how talented she was. Tamara would glance at him and immediately go back to whatever she had been doing. "I thought you weren't getting back until Wednesday," she'd say, not really expecting an answer and not caring if she got one. After that she would ignore him. He'd take her out to dinner later, perhaps a show at Heinz Hall; bribery had long ago proven the quickest and surest way to her heart.

"Looks like it might rain," said the cabby, and indeed, it was only a moment later that Jacque heard the rhythmic tapping of raindrops against the windshield, starting off slow, then growing into a steady drizzle that blanketed the city outside.

"Seems like it's always raining here," said Jacque.

"Tell me about it. But," he shrugged, "it wouldn't be home if it didn't rain once in a while, you know?

Jacque was somewhat dismayed, as the cab turned onto Linden Street to find Tamara's car sitting in the driveway. There would be no time to prepare, then – no time, either, to change his mind. He paid the driver and hoisted his bags from the trunk, stumbling somewhat as he climbed the narrow steps leading up to his porch. All up and down the street the front windows of the houses were lit, their quiet glow reassuring him somehow.

He paused in front of the door and looked through his own window: Tamara, he could see, was seated on the couch; in front of her, on the floor, was Marguerite. Mother was brushing daughter's hair, a second-rate Movie of the Week blaring away on the television. Jacque took a deep breath and sighed. Thirty-two was old for tennis, he thought, but not for life. He would do his best with what he had. Love was a choice, after all, not fate or fountains or even Paris. Bracing himself, he twisted the doorknob and stepped inside.

I Do and Do and Do
Sue Eisenfeld

am getting married again. This must be the tenth time – I've lost track. One year it was in San Francisco, another time in Florida, twice this year in Maryland.

I'm marrying the same man, of course, again and again as we travel across the country attending weddings. In the city, on the coast, on a mountaintop – while our eyes fill with joyful tears for our friends and relatives who are taking the plunge, we are getting married all over again.

Some of our remarriages happen through music. We hired a glass-harp player for our wedding – one of the few people in the world who plays this unusual instrument – but he didn't know how to play the piece I'd always dreamed of walking down the aisle to: Pachelbel's *Canon in D*. We settled for Beethoven's "Ode to Joy," but we haven't let go of the canon as our true wedding music. Now, when we hear it, we squeeze hands, turning to each other with eyes that say, "At last!"

Part of the joy in adopting other people's weddings is that we get to have all the things we didn't have: a receiving line, dancing, a real wedding dress. Seven years ago when we said, "I do," we kept it simple: an off-the-rack dress and my uncoifed long hair, lawn games, a Ben & Jerry's feast at a bed-and-breakfast with Blue Ridge views – then off to our honeymoon the next day.

I was a different person then. I didn't want dancing because I was uncomfortable in my own skin. There were no bridesmaids because I didn't want to have to ask anyone for help. And I didn't want the more recent tradition of a next-day brunch because I was too stressed.

The person I am now loves to dance – at weddings, at concerts, in my own living room. It's the best part of any occasion. In the years since my wedding, I've reached out more to my community of friends. Asking them for help with the wedding would have been a way of inviting them into my new life with my husband. I'm also more practical and low-key. Instead of planning a catered brunch, which we couldn't have afforded after the wedding and reception, bagels in our back yard would have been fine. I couldn't see that then.

―◇―

Most of our marriage renewals happen through the vows and readings. We watch others walk down the aisle, and we listen to the words – "friendship that has caught fire," "the quiet understanding, mutual confidence, sharing and forgiving," "love as patience and kindness." These blessings reaffirm the way my husband and I have been with each other in the past seven years. They tell us we've selected the right priorities and headed in the right direction.

Sometimes we recognize a reading as one from our own ceremony: Kahlil Gibran's "On Marriage," the Apache wedding prayer, an Irish blessing. We're reminded of our choice "to give our hearts, but not into each other's keeping," "to fill each other's cup, but drink not from one cup," and to be "shelter and warmth to the other." We remember our day, that glorious fall afternoon.

So when my husband leads me to the dance floor in Chicago, or when I am asked to speak at my best friend's ceremony in Sandy Spring, Maryland, or when I introduce myself to an old friend's parents at a wedding on Long Island, I cherish the moment. I bask in the bond I feel with the newlyweds and their families. I reflect on how far I've traveled since my wedding. And I vow all over again to love, cherish, and respect my husband for the rest of my days, in good times and bad, in sickness and in health. Especially at weddings.

Cloud Burst
Robert Klein Engler

Look at this world with its beat
of storms. I am in the midst of fog
with rain and wind, then heat.
I did not plan this dialogue,

those skinny hands or freckled glow.
Such a fool I am. Everyone knows.
While others sail, I still row.
Tossed around by love, I love it so.

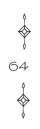

64

Aaron and Faulkner
Bertil Falk

t was not as she remembered it. Instead of an Automat, there was a Burger King. And that Nasdaq thing obviously wanted to take over Times Square. There were no bums at sight on The Bowery. Worst of all, her favorite antiquarian bookshop was gone. Lillith Steinbaum felt taken in. New York City was not as she remembered it. She had not even touched on the idea that 35 years of absence would mean changes on such a scale. Standing on the sidewalk looking at the record shop in a new building where once had been a wonderful second-hand bookshop in a dilapidated edifice, she realized that Mr. Henderson probably had gone to the happy hunting grounds of bibliophiles. He must have been poised on the brink of the grave even then. His nervous lips, that gray temple, the slowness of his eyes, those shaky hands that barely could hold a book for five seconds. She had never thought of it before, but he must have been in the process of dying in front of her, while he produced that Faulkner novel she had been after 35 years earlier. *Requiem for a Nun.* All these years she remembered the piles of back issues of old pulps and slicks looking as if they would topple over any second. But they never did. They had always looked the same. As had Mr. Henderson himself wringing his trembling hands and asking, 'What can I do for you, Miss .....?" He always forgot her name and she always filled in, 'Steinbaum. Lillith Steinbaum.'

When she was 20, she was adamant that she would become Mrs. Aaron Eisensturm. When she was 23, she was still confident of that. At the age of 25 and one year after Aaron married Lidia Gabor in Queens, she was not so sure any more. But it took another year until the full significance of that wedding dawned on her and yet another year before it had sunk in. At least in a way – though some kind of hope lingered on.

Her mother's illness saved her. There could be no question of leaving Mom to her fate like a recluse at a nursing home. Lillith had given her notice and left New York City on a Greyhound bound for LA. She was 26 then and she never again worked as an editor at a publishing firm. She never again worked at all unless taking care of a nearly helpless mother is considered work. Her mother's pensions and benefits were actually more than they needed. And those IBM stocks Lillith had inherited from her father reproduced like rabbits over the years and yielded a good return. She spent most of her spare time reading novels and dreaming of Aaron. The day she reached 31, she learned he had died of cancer over there in Queens, and that Lidia had remarried. For some reason that stimulated her fantasies rather than ended them.

She thought that she recalled his looks but without realizing it, Aaron changed in her imagination – for the better. He became more and more good-looking and thoughtful. She would shut her eyes and pass her hand over his dark hair and kiss his shapely ear lobe. His once glassy look became a brown, considerate gaze. Aaron had never been such an attractive and charming man as he matured into five years after his death.

Aaron's favorite writer was William Faulkner. She had never withheld that her weakness for the author was a consequence of her impressive crush on Aaron. Crush may seem to be a vague designation of something more like obsession, but if one imagines a crush covering forty years without being weakened, that is impressive, isn't it? And not exactly an obsession, but rather a harmless habit. The kind of crush that loves are made of, Shakespeare could have told her – or Ibsen for that matter. Both as dead as Aaron and Faulkner.

The thing is that Lillith, in spite of what you may think of her, was not at all pathetic. She was not prone to self-pity or feelings of inferiority. And above all, she was not depressed because of Aaron's choice. Unlike the disappointed ones who mourned their misfired visions, hers was an existence of fulfillment simply because her unrealized wedding to Aaron lent a certain firmness to her life; a backbone.

Caring for her ailing mother was not a burden either. On the contrary, her mother was a bundle of *joie de vivre*, spending her days playing solitaire on her computer and cracking jokes, many of them pertaining to the blessing of unmarried daughters and their infidel expectations. And Lillith smiled, knowing that her mother loved her so much that she wished her married to Aaron – or to anyone for that matter – a hundred times.

Lillith was a regular visitor to the local library and became a friend of the librarian, Edward G. Redstone, a tall booklover. His towering form threw fascinating shadows across the bookshelves when he slowly walked from his counter to pick up some obscure volume or best-seller. These shadows were the consequence of the fluorescent tubes, the strange arrangement of which puzzled most first-time visitors there. He was a serious man with a serious smile and he took a serious interest in Lillith.

They would spend hours together discussing literature, especially William Faulkner. Edward told her that when Howard Hawks adapted *The Big Sleep* for the screen, Faulkner wrote the manuscript, together with newcomer Leigh Brackett. She was young and curious and spent a lot of time on the lot during the shooting. One day Humphrey Bogart came over to her, showed her a page of the manuscript and said, "Did you write this sentence? It's impossible to say!" Leigh Brackett's commentary when she later told the story was, "Faulkner wrote Faulkner prose and that was wonderful in Faulkner's books, but his sentences did not fit as cues. That is why Faulkner goes into film history as the scriptwriter who never got one single sentence through without alterations in Hollywood."

Lillith reacted vehemently against this story. "But it's true," Edward said and after that they had half a year of discussions about Faulkner's language and the failure of Hollywood in general and Bogart in particular to appreciate a great American Nobel Prize winner. ("But Bogart could not possibly know at that stage that Faulkner would be awarded the prize," Edward argued.) But more important, it led to Lillith's discovery that Faulkner had written for *Ellery Queen's Mystery Magazine.*

"In 1946, one of his stories actually won a second prize in a short story competition in *Ellery Queen's Mystery Magazine*," Edward told her. "I always wanted to find a copy of that particular issue."

Lillith was shocked when Edward one day out of thin air proposed to her. The very idea that someone else than Aaron would ... well, it was just alien to her. From her wheelchair, her mother anxiously encouraged an alliance. Now, Lillith had nothing against him. He was a nice man. He had read everything by Faulkner he could lay his hands on, with the exception of that *Ellery Queen's Mystery Magazine* story and a few other things. He would probably have become a good husband. But to marry someone else was out of question. Somehow both her mother and Edward came to understand and accept, and life went on as usual.

When her mother died after many years, most of them spent in that wheelchair, Lillith was 61. Edward G. Redstone was the only one who came to the funeral, for even though Lillith had turned him down, they continued to see each other on a regular basis and discuss the more profound passages of *Ulysses* or the latest achievements of Norman Mailer, though they avoided discussing Faulkner. After the funeral they had a sundae at Howard Johnson's somewhere near Hollywood and Vine. It was when Edward G. Redstone said, "Now you're free to do whatever you want," that Lillith Steinbaum made up her mind. She decided to return to New York City and Queens.

The day she went, Edward accompanied her to the airport where they had lunch together at the revolving restaurant. She descended on Edison Hotel at 228 West 47th, just around the corner of Times Square, appreciated the Art Deco lobby and had a shower. Then she went walking down Broadway in the direction of downtown to pick up that Faulkner back issue of *Ellery Queen's Mystery Magazine* she was cocksure that Mr. Henderson would produce out of his piles of magazines. It was then she found out – to her sincere surprise – that her favorite second-to-none second-hand bookshop was gone.

Jay Leno's vulgar and spiteful remarks delivered with a sunny temperament did not cheer her up that night. Neither did David Letterman's self-destructive treatment of his own show. So she switched it off, pondering over her past and her life. Yes, she had discussed things like that with Edward in an artificial way over the years, but the replacement of an Automat with a Burger King added existential thoughts to her imagination. It was that night, just before she fell asleep, that she decided to visit the grave.

The lady in charge at the cemetery in Queens was very helpful. After five minutes, Lillith knew the grave number and its exact location on the cemetery map. But when she came to the burial place, there was nothing to see except a grassy space, no stone, no name. Not even the grave number was displayed. Not far away was an open pit and beside it a small excavator with a coffin-broad dipper. The gravedigger was lying outstretched on the lawn, reading a pocket-sized book, yellowed with age. He was about 50, his smile of that everlasting kind that never disappears from a face because it is an integrated part of its constitution.

"Excuse me, but why have they taken away Aaron Eisensturm's gravestone?" Her question had a distinct ring of accusation.

The man came to his feet. "Who?"

"Aaron Eisensturm. He's supposed to be buried here." She pointed at the spot where Aaron was supposed to spend the remaining part of eternity.

"There has never been a gravestone there," he said.

"How do you know?"

"I've been here all my life. My father worked here before me, his father before him. There has never been a gravestone there."

She should have known. No Automat restaurant, no bums, barely any Bowery, no bookshop, no Mr. Henderson, no *Ellery Queen's Mystery Magazine.* And now, no gravestone. Could that Lidia have been so insensitive, tight-fisted and mean that she had refused the expense of a gravestone for her husband?

Lillith did not know the answer. She suddenly felt very tired. What was the use of this? Aaron did not even have a gravestone. He could as well be dead, or alive for that matter. This was ridiculous. She was ridiculous.

The grave worker stood there with his book.

Lillith softened at the sight. He looked so frail. Not like a person employed in the vicinity of Death.

He said, "I remember the interment of ... what was his name?"

"Aaron Eisensturm."

"Ironstorm," he translated with a murmuring tone and it sounded like the name of a comic book hero to Lillith. "No, I can't remember that name, but I remember many years ago when a coffin was lowered down there where you're standing right now. In those days there were no excavators tailor-made for grave digging. We used spades. I must have been 17 or so. I used to help my father when he dug. There was the normal crowd of mourners."

69

"After so many years and funerals, how can you possibly remember this particular burial?"

"I've a good memory. Show any spot in this graveyard and I'll remember at least something. It's as if seeing a spot triggers memories."

He was, of course, right, she thought. Places triggered recollections, as did smells.

"What else do you remember from that interment?"

"Nothing specific. The coffin was lowered, people cried and threw flowers on top of it. A very ordinary thing."

"What are you reading?" She changed subject for no reason at all. Or perhaps she asked the question in order to have something to say that made the world go around again.

"Faulkner."

"Faulkner?" She looked at him with different eyes.

"William Faulkner," he said. "You know, there is really no big difference between digging graves and digging Faulkner."

He showed her his digest-sized magazine. The cover had once

been blue, but it must have been sunbathing for the color had faded.

"Can you imagine?" he said. "Faulkner wrote for this mystery magazine. It's No. 31 of *Ellery Queen's Mystery Magazine,* June 1946."

Lillith had heard of revelations, but she had never before stumbled upon one. His words magnetized her into bargaining and she returned to LA in triumph. It took her less than 60 seconds to become Mrs. Edward G. Redstone in Las Vegas. They spent their honeymoon on the beach of Waikiki, and every evening for the rest of her life, she relaxed while the soothing voice of her husband read aloud from some good book, preferably by Faulkner.

Il-Logic

Lynn Fitzgerald

He can only imagine the world
She walks or wears her hair in
Love is a deprivation of sorts, like beauty
Some logic lost, an interruption of integrity.
She can only imagine the world
He walks and wears his glasses in
Or how he doesn't look at life but does.

Yet she knows how his hands feel
How definite the grasp
And this holds fast the dream,
The arm reaches with the fingers for the pen
The wrist supports the words.

Is this a poem or is it life?
The man stretches his dark coat across
His shoulders, walks through the doorway
Into his world and the woman steps
Inside her life, silent as a leaf falling to ground.

The Fisherman Gets Home
Maureen Tolman Flannery

These days he navigates as a stranger
the contraptions of his own tackle box.
This time now he must master anew
the tricky skill of using his own reel
as the line balls up and tangles and confounds.
With infinite patience he unwinds
what his palsied fingers continue to enmesh.
His few remaining teeth bite
a lead sinker tight around the line.
He squashes a grabbed grasshopper

onto a hook he can hardly see,
shuffles to the water's edge,
and is a happy man.

Our Glass for Martin, 1968
Pat Gallant

I am but half today
yet not a day has passed in full
since I was last with you.
But still, I have become but a weak light
in the short skies of one day's time
feeling each sand drop
one
by
one
grain
by
grain
rolling silently
along a glass hour.
My mind cannot seek comfort
for it plays elusive games with me.
It is with you that comfort lies.
So, I walk as if in search of one half
that is not –
– yet is
so much myself. Better for me is that
kind hand that reaches for mine,
that melts your warmth into my soul,
Oh,
for it is then that I am whole

Dance Date
Barbara Goldowsky

I have a date with Fred.
I'll pick him up in that crowded
back room. He's waiting patiently –
or maybe not – he's probably
restless, tapping his cane,
starting to walk up the walls.

He wants to bring Ginger, he says.
That's OK, she can show me some
tricks – for instance, just between us
girls – how do you do those kicks
and twirls without losing your skirt?

Don't worry, Fred, I'm on my way.
I'll take you home and turn you on,
and I'll pay for your time. It's really
all right – I can keep you
all night –

my gigolo on video.

Autumn Rose
Phil Gruis

A rose burst
from autumn grass
to feel the sun's
last warm touch.

Furious night
hurled its cloak of cold.

The rose tightened to a fist
fought
but died in the dark.

He pressed it in a book.

Each winter day
he opens the book
to warm his trembling hands.

76

The Ivory Satin Robe
Mary Ann Grzych

Marie stood before the mirror turning left, then right, peering over her shoulder, hands pressing against her stomach as she sucked in a deep breath. Behind her the bed was littered with skirts, blouses, sweaters and slacks tried on and discarded.

Why am I doing this? she thought, seeing her reflection in the mirror. I haven't had a date since Eisenhower was President. It's like being a teenager again, except my hair is gray instead of blonde, there's a few wrinkles in my face, extra inches around my waist, and my father won't be waiting up for me when I get home. Will I have to ask him in? Will he want to come in? What if he tries to kiss me? What if he doesn't? God, I *am* a teenager again!

It's just lunch, Marie thought. A casual sweater and a pair of slacks, and I'll let it go at that. She sighed, almost regretting she'd seen him at the library the day before and had offered an ear – why am I so worried – he's got a pot belly and a comb-over, for God's sake.

Ted showed up promptly at noon in neatly pressed twill slacks, a plaid shirt and leather jacket, shoes shined, and his salt & pepper comb-over neatly slicked down. They drove to one of her favorite restaurants and didn't speak of Sally, the warm, talented woman who'd been his wife and Marie's art student and friend – dead three months now – though Marie knew they would.

Over lunch, they shared a lot about how much they missed Sally and her Ralph, dead four years. Later, while strolling through a nearby park, it seemed natural for Ted to take Marie's hand as they continued their conversation. The date ended at Marie's door with Ted saying he'd call soon, which turned out to be the next morning.

"Let me take you to dinner tonight."

She hesitated briefly, but agreed. The next two days were much the same. Ted would call in the morning and ask her to dinner that night. Marie tried to slow things down, but he pleaded and she always relented. "He's lonely," she told herself. "And I do enjoy our evenings." After dinner they wound up back at Marie's house watching TV, Ted holding her hand as they sat on the couch.

A few weeks later, Ted asked Marie to accompany him on a trip to central Ohio to visit Sally's sister, Linda. "The trees are beautiful there in late October," he said. "You'll love it."

"Won't Linda resent having me there so soon...?"

"No, I told her that I might be bringing someone along. You would have your own bedroom," he assured her. "We could get an early start if you would stay at my place the night before. With your own room and bath, of course," he added. When she arrived that evening, he ceremoniously presented her with a new, ivory satin, lace-trimmed robe. "It's only for here," he said. "You can't take it home with you."

Marie was stunned, not only by the gift, but by the conditions that went with it. She certainly wasn't ready for Ted's assumptions.

"I brought my own," she replied, handing back the satin robe. "And I'll leave the towels here, too."

Ted forced a laugh, ignoring the edge in her voice, but not missing the way she touched the luxurious garment with more than a hint of regret.

—◇—

Ohio was truly beautiful in October. Each curve in the road brought a scene more spectacular than the last. Sunshine touching the trees highlighted brilliant reds and yellows, turned russet so deep the leaves looked like fine mahogany leather. They drove with soft music playing; the tiny whistle of the wind as it swept past the car window the only other sound. Conversation was unnecessary. Almost too soon they were pulling into Linda's driveway.

The house immediately put Marie at ease. A large porch, filled with wicker chairs and tables, stretched across the front of a white country cottage. The yard was full of late roses, ornamental grasses, and colorful mums. Linda clearly shared Sally's love of gardening. A hammock still hung between two huge maple trees. It looked like the cover of *Country Living* magazine. Linda must have heard their car because she was out the door to greet them before the engine was turned off.

"I've got a fresh pot of coffee on and some banana bread just out of the oven," Linda said. "You must be Marie. Sally's told me so much about you through the years; I feel like I know you already."

As warm and friendly as Sally, Linda greeted Marie with a hug and made her feel at home the minute they walked through the door. The guest room was bright and cheery. Sunshine coming through the window traced a golden path on the bare oak floor to an antique Jenny Lind bed covered with a handmade, patchwork quilt and lots of soft, puffy pillows. A rose pattern lamp on the bedside table looked antique, as did the cane back Lincoln rocker in the corner. The attached bath was modern, but the fixtures had been chosen with an eye to days gone by. The toilet had a chain flush from an overhead tank and the tub sat on claw feet. Fluffy pink towels lay across the rim and a bar of scented gel soap filled the soap dish. Everything in the suite had been chosen to make a visitor feel welcome. Marie did.

That evening the three of them stayed up late drinking coffee at the kitchen table, sharing memories of Sally. The next morning, Marie went outside to sketch the house while Ted and Linda talked. I can make some note cards when we get home and send them to Linda as a thank-you for her hospitality, she thought. They had lunch at a good restaurant in an old brewery building in town. Marie loved the vintage houses and storefronts. "I wish I had time to draw some of them," she said.

"Come again, and stay longer," Linda urged.

Ted laughed and chatted with Marie as the miles home flew by, and before she knew it, he was transferring her suitcase from his Volvo into her Escort. "I'm so glad you came with me," he said.

"I am, too. I had a great time."

Taking her into his arms, Ted gave Marie a long kiss. "We'll have to do it again sometime," he said, hopefully.

She got in her car so he wouldn't notice the excited flush of her cheeks. Marie was so flustered by the lingering sensation of his kiss that she turned the wrong way at the end of the block. God, I hope he didn't see that, she thought.

Ted called Marie every day, and soon after their return from Ohio, he invited her to a party with his "snowbird camper" friends: people he'd met because he had a luxurious RV, a home-on-wheels he and Sally drove to Texas each winter.

Marie enjoyed the party, feeling attractive in a blue slack suit and colorful shawl. Her eyes sparkled when Ted proudly introduced her to his friends. The men seemed to nod their approval to him and everyone made her welcome, except Ellen, a widow, who glared at Marie when she thought no one was watching.

"How'd you like the gang?" Ted asked eagerly on their way home.

"They seem like a lively bunch."

"They are," Ted said, turning in the seat and smiling at her. "Why don't you come to Texas with me this winter? You know I'm falling for you. We'll have a great time and I want to show you all my favorite places down there."

"I'm not going to do that," Marie answered firmly. "Even if I wanted to, I can't be gone all winter. I have family and friends here and art classes to teach, but you should go," she said, reaching over to touch his arm.

"I hate the cold Chicago winter, but I don't want to go alone," he sighed. "Guess I'll have to store the RV for the winter. Will you at least go to Rockford with me next Tuesday to have it winterized? We'll tow my car and drive back after lunch."

Marie agreed, and on Tuesday Ted proudly gave her a tour of the RV before they left. The sitting room was outfitted with comfortable leather furniture and a large color TV. The adjacent kitchen-dining area boasted gleaming oak cabinets and stainless steel appliances. A bath, complete with shower, separated the living area from a large bedroom with a king-size bed and oak dressers. They were barely out of the driveway when Ted turned to her with an eager smile on his face. "Well, how do you like this?" he asked, jiggling anxiously in the seat.

Marie tensed, crossed her arms and continued to look straight ahead. "It's fine, Ted, but I'm not going to Texas with you."

"Okay," he mumbled, slumping back in his seat. Marie quickly changed the subject to where they were going for lunch.

—◆—

The phone calls and dates continued into early December. They usually went out for lunch or dinner, then watched TV at her house, sitting on the couch in her small living room, holding hands and kissing a little when she allowed it.

"How are things going with Ted?" her friend, Ann, asked one day.

"A little too fast for me. You know what happened last week? We were sitting on the couch at my house watching TV when he turned to me out of the blue and said, 'What'da ya think of sex?' I almost choked!"

"What did you say?"

"I asked if he was any good at it"

Ann burst our laughing. "What did he say?" she asked when she finally got control of herself.

"'Ummm, not very.'" Another fit of laughter convulsed them both.

"You can't tell anyone about that," Marie said. "Not a soul. Promise!"

"OK, but that's going to be really hard, you know," Ann replied, still giggling as Marie quieted, realizing that she wasn't at all ready to take that leap.

—◆—

Soon the weather chilled and everyone was caught up in plans for Christmas. Marie's daughter, Rita, called one day to confirm their early Christmas celebration at her house. "I hardly see you anymore, Mom," she said. "I miss our outings on my day off."

"I know. I miss you, too. I'm trying to cool it a little, but Ted just wants to go everywhere with me. He's even jealous of my cat. Wants to know why I keep the old thing around. He shouldn't be so quick to want to get rid of old things. He's no spring chicken himself."

"Should I invite him to our family Christmas party next Sunday?" Rita asked.

Marie felt her lips tighten as she hesitated. "Yes. I think it'd be a nice thing to do. It's his first Christmas without Sally."

The day of the party Ted showed up at Marie's with unwrapped cheese tray gifts for her three kids, leaving her to scramble at the last minute to find wrapping paper. They arrived at Rita's barely in time for dinner. He was pleasant but quiet during the meal, and right after all the gifts had been exchanged – including the tin of cookies she'd baked for him and his Barnes & Noble gift card to her – Ted turned to Marie and said, "Let's go."

Marie stiffened in her seat. "I don't want to leave yet," she protested, frowning.

81

When Ted insisted, Marie reluctantly agreed. "I'm sorry that I told you to invite him," she whispered to Rita as they said good-bye.

Outside Marie said sharply, "The next time you have to leave early, let me know and we'll both drive. I wanted to spend more time with my family."

Ted was quiet in the car. When they got home, he helped her carry her presents to the door, gave her a quick good night peck on the cheek, and left. Marie thought it was strange since he always came in, but she gave it no more thought until Tuesday night, when he hadn't phoned. That was unusual. He'd been calling at least once a day since they started dating. By Thursday, Marie wondered if she'd upset him, so she called him – a first.

"Have I done something to offend you?" she asked, her voice rising apprehensively.

"No, I've just been busy," he replied.

Relieved, Marie said, "Well, I thought I should ask when we'll pick up the RV."

After a pause, Ted replied, "Actually...Ellen's going with me." He fell silent for another long moment. "We're leaving for Texas the day after Christmas..." He finished in a breathless rush of jumbled words. "And by the way, she moved in with me."

Marie was speechless for a moment. "When did this happen and when were you going to tell me about it?" she asked, picturing Ellen in the ivory satin bathrobe.

"A few days ago," Ted said. "She's been going to Texas with the gang for years and even went last year after her husband died. She has a spot reserved that we can use. We're taking my RV."

Afterward, Marie thought of all the things she should have said to Ted. A few weeks ago he'd been falling for her, and suddenly Ellen's moved in!

She got her chance when he called that evening.

"You sounded mad at me when I told you about Ellen," he said.

"I was, but not because she's going to Texas with you. I told you to go, and if you found someone to go with, then good for you. I'm mad because you didn't have the decency to tell me. You owed me that, at least. Sunday you're at my daughter's Christmas party with me, and a few days later, you tell me that Ellen moved in with you. Of course I'm mad!"

"You're right," Ted apologized. "I guess I should have said something sooner."

Marie tossed and turned in bed that night feeling betrayal and loss, yet relief that it was over.

The next morning she was making breakfast when the phone rang. "How about lunch with me today?" Ted asked.

Silence.

"Then how about dinner?"

"Are you nuts?" Marie shouted into the phone. "What's wrong with you? I'm not going to lunch or dinner with you today, or any other day!"

"Sorry," Ted said, then added, "I should have told you sooner, and I should have given you that robe, too. I knew you liked it, and now it's..." His resonant sigh suggested a groan. "Well...have a nice Christmas."

Marie pictured Ellen in the luxury of that robe, slammed down the phone, and muttered out loud, "He's either the dumbest man ever, or just plain nervy! Or both. I'm glad he hates the cold." As she contemplated the Chicago winter she would face, Marie looked out and thought she saw the first flakes fall.

How Foolish
Carol Haggas

How foolish they were;
how young and terribly careless,
squandering love so recklessly
on the promise of other faces,
the collision with other worlds.
He moved out, she moved out;
still, she brought him flowers,
and he – he was always her rock.
I'm going to New Jersey, he said.
She surprised him: I'd like to come too.
And so they moved on and on,
and on a moving train late one night
after some thirty years had gone by,
her gray head on his shoulder,
a smile on his still youthful face,
the conducter said:
you're the only happy man on this train.
That's 'cause you're with me,
he whispered in her ear,
which wasn't at all a foolish thing to say,
since they were no longer young,
and they were terribly, terribly careful now
not to squander love.

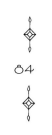

84

What I Know about Love
Melanie Hammer

Before I even say anything, you should know that I'm a sophisticated, liberal woman. I live in the Village, OK? A couple of my friends are gay men, and I won't insult you or them by proclaiming that they're my best friends. I'm telling you this up front so it'll be clear I don't have anything against homosexuals. I just think Dana should have figured out this lesbian thing before she got herself a husband and kids.

If it was just that she was leaving Jay, I'd have understood completely. Of course, I would have worried about the children, but truthfully, I never thought Jay was that great. A sweet guy, put in his time with the kids and the household labor, but not all that bright. If you ask me, he's a walking warning about the cumulative effects of marijuana, but what do I know? Maybe he was always absent-minded. He didn't have any drive. I'm a good mother, so I never told Dana that I thought Jay was a little *nebbish*. I hid my true feelings about him. I'm good at that. I've had a lot of practice. They produced two beautiful kids, I'll say that for them. They had a decent house and they liked their jobs, but I always knew there was something missing. So when Dana came over to tell me they were separating, my first reaction was, it's about time. Then I asked about my grandchildren.

Dana had an answer for everything. Claire and Evan would stay in the house with Jay, and they'd worked out how often she'd see them, child care payments, all the details. What kind of daughter leaves her husband and children and doesn't even mention it to her mother until she's all packed, with one foot out the door? But Dana was always like that.

I'll only be six blocks away, she said. They'll still be raised by two parents. Like it should be that simple. She sat on my new beige sectional, swinging one leg crossed over the other, like someone expecting to get everything she wanted. I took a good look at her, new haircut, pretty, with that glow I've seen before. *I knew.* Are you seeing anyone, I asked her, and she got all coy. Yes, she said. Who? I said. A cute, smart Jewish professor at Brooklyn College, she said. I'd have hoped for a private college myself, a university, maybe, but you can't have everything. It sounded like a step up from Jay. And how old is this nice, smart Jewish professor, I asked. She's 41, Dana said. *No,* I said, but I had my wits about me enough that I didn't say any more. She remembers every bad thing I say, and none of the good. Her brother Randall's the same way; as much as I've done for them, they still resent me.

Dana has an apartment near the children now, and she sees them nearly every day. They sleep over by her place twice a week, and she stops at their house every morning to take Evan to school. Often, when I call in the afternoons, she's there, doing the homework and snack duty until Jay gets home. I can't honestly say she ran out on her children, but it's a big change. She thinks they're adjusting, but I know how much it hurts them.

Jay and I talk at least once a week. Mostly it's to make arrangements for me to see the children, but I'm a good listener, too. I'm the grandmother; I'm staying in their lives. I can even come up with some sympathy for Jay. He's not much of a man, but he didn't deserve this.

Dana hasn't told the children about her lifestyle change yet, just that she and Jay didn't love each other any more like mommies and daddies should. She said, hey, why give them everything at once, your parents are splitting up and your mother's a dyke? Let them deal with one thing at a time, let them get to know Beryl, and gradually, they'll know everything. But she can't fool me. Dana hasn't told them the whole story because, deep in her heart, she knows what I know: it won't last. I don't care how happy she is, people just don't change like that. She's 43 years old. If she were really a lesbian, she would've been one already. This is just your standard mid-life crisis, all dressed up in some idea she has about love.

Of course, I'd like to see her happy. I'm her mother. And I don't have anything against true love, either. Even at my age, with everything I've seen, I'll admit I still think it exists, somewhere. If two people are really lucky.

When I was a girl back in Kansas City, I fell in love with a guy from Oklahoma. His family had business connections with mine, and he used to come to town every few weeks. Aaron was tall, over six feet, and just the kind of man I liked to go out with, the kind who was interested in what I had to say and what I wanted to do. He wore cowboy boots all the time, even with a suit. I wrote him every day when we weren't together, and he wrote me once or twice a week. I thought: *He's the one. I'll graduate high school and marry Aaron Reitman and I'll go off to Oklahoma with him and be perfectly happy.* That's what we wanted in those days. It's what I wanted.

Then the letters stopped coming. I wrote him the usual supplications – are you mad at me, is it something I've done, I'm sorry. Please, Aaron. I called his house two or three times, but they always said he was on the road. His brother Sol came to Kansas City to do business after that, but nobody could find out anything for me. One afternoon, I made up my face and put on a nice pair of slacks and a new belted jacket I had – not a dress because I didn't want to look like I was trying too hard – and I rode downtown with my cousin Jake. I was at the store when Sol came in. He hesitated in the doorway when he saw me, blinked at me across the glass cases of gold and jewels. Then I said hello, and so did he. How's Aaron, I said, casually. I'd practiced saying his name thousands of times till I could do it naturally, just another word, two syllables and it's done. He's fine, Sol said. He wouldn't look me in the eye. I'm sorry, Isabel, he mumbled. Nothing to be sorry for, I said. Tell him I said hi. I sauntered out of the store like I was any carefree high school girl, walked to Swope Park, and sat down and cried until I couldn't squeeze out one more tear. Then I picked myself up and went home. I was glad I hadn't given him any more of myself than I had.

I married Henry Rothbart two years later, when I was nearly 20. I can't say it was on the rebound; I'd dated other guys. I didn't love Henry the way I'd loved Aaron, but I figured I wasn't a baby any more, either. And I'm not sorry I married him; he got me out of Kansas City and we had three children. I loved them so much when they were little; when I was 24 I had three children under the age of four and we all had the best time together. Dana says she doesn't see how I did it – she spaced hers four years apart – but she just doesn't get it. I loved being a mother. I was good at it. I didn't want anything for myself. And when my marriage went bad, at least I waited until my kids were grown before I got divorced.

Henry and I had been separated for about six months, not even divorced yet, when my phone rang one night. Hello? I said. Hello, a man's voice said, and I knew who it was.

I let Aaron take me to dinner. It had been almost 40 years, what was the point of bearing a grudge? Besides, I was curious. I haven't aged as badly as some; I put on a black skirt that came to just above the knee, sheer hose and heels. I still have good legs, and I know how to show them off without looking foolish, the way some women my age show too much of their chicken legs. They should know better. When I looked in the mirror before I left, I knew Aaron would still find me attractive.

He stood up when I came into the restaurant. I couldn't quite read his expression– smiling, but ready to cry, too, maybe. He wasn't much different, curly hair gone a little gray, a few more lines around his mouth, a little softer around the jaw. He was still wearing cowboy boots. When he pulled out a chair for me to sit, I saw his wedding ring.

We did the preliminaries, told each other how good we looked, ordered drinks, and then Aaron took a deep breath.

"Is," he said. "Isabel. I wronged you some years ago and I want to try to explain myself. Not that I expect you to forgive me, but it's been eating me up inside. I feel like I owe you an explanation for the way I acted. If you'll allow me."

"I have wondered about you once or twice over the years," I said.

He flinched, and I reached out and patted his hand. He curled his fingers around mine, and I didn't pull away.

"You were so young and beautiful, Is," he said. "And you're still beautiful."

"Though not so young?" I said, and he chuckled.

"We're not old, Is. Maybe not as young as we were, but young enough. Back then, I wanted to give you everything. I wanted to ask you to marry me. But I couldn't. I knew you wanted to have children. Do you remember me talking about my brother Reuben?"

"I never met him. He was in a home when I first knew you."

He nodded.

"We didn't know what was wrong with him. I thought, what if it's in my blood? What if I give Isabel a child like that?"

"You never said any of that to me."

He took a long swallow of his drink.

"I was afraid you would have talked me into taking our chances."

I nodded towards the ring on his hand.

"Apparently, someone else had the opportunity."

He squeezed my hand tighter.

"That was later. You were already married to Henry. You were in New York, you had kids. By the time I married Helene, I was older, not so scared. But I was also older, not so in love. Tell me you've had a good life, Isabel. Tell me you've been happy."

I took a swallow of my wine, thinking about how to answer him.

"I've had a good run," I said finally. "I can't complain."

"I've done all right, too," he said. "But I never loved Helene the way I loved you. I've missed you, Is."

"I never loved Henry the way I loved you, either," I said. "You idiot."

Aaron was in town for the rest of the week, and we were together for all of the time when he wasn't at meetings. I felt cheap being with him at his hotel, so I had him at my apartment, where we could feel like we were at home together. At the end of the week, when he had to go back, we were both clear about what we wanted: he would tell his wife about us and ask her for a divorce. He'd come back to see me as soon as he could, and we'd start to make arrangements for me to move out to Phoenix, where he was living. He'd made a big mistake, but after all these years, he was going to fix it. We were going to get to be together the way we always should have been. It wouldn't be like I had never married Henry, of course, but I was going to get to go back to a place in my life and choose again. Or be chosen. I knew I was capable of having a warm, loving, fulfilling relationship; maybe Henry wasn't, but I was. I woke up happy every day, grateful to have the chance to try again, loving Aaron and knowing he loved me. We weren't too old to start over.

You'd think I would've been old enough to know better. I was 55, not that much older than Dana is now. I plunged in anyway. And I know Aaron loved me, both times. He was just weak. He kept saying he would tell his wife soon, after the youngest got accepted to college, after she graduated high school, after they packed her off, but the months dragged on and he didn't. Finally, I said, tell Helene by New Year's or we're through. As much as I loved him, I wasn't going to hang on by my fingernails to the edges of Aaron when I was ready to change my whole life for him. It was all or nothing for me. And then it was nothing, and I'd had my heart thoroughly broken twice in one lifetime by the same man.

So when Dana picked herself up and moved out of the house where she'd lived with her husband and kids, you think I didn't understand? After all, I married a man I never truly loved; I once was willing to reconstruct my world for someone I loved completely, and who I believed loved me back the same way. But not like this. This is one of Dana's experiments, a temporary distraction. What could they make together?

When I call Dana, I ask about her apartment, tell her I worry about whether she can handle this schedule, the pressure. We chat about the children. I don't ask about the girlfriend; why should I? I know I'll be around long after this relationship ends. I've been here before.

90

Maggie's Wedding Day
Susan Hannus

After the invitation came, Maggie spent weeks and hundreds of dollars at the spa trying to remove 20 years. She joined a health club and sweated off 25 lbs. But tonight, she turned the lights out and pulled the covers around her, thoughts of *Steve* escorting her into dreamland. Tomorrow they were to be married.

He'd been her high school sweetheart, the one she let get away. No man ever lived up to her memory of Steve. As she'd mailed the *RSVP* for her 20th high school reunion, her heartbeat quickened.

The big night arrived like a fairytale. Their eyes met and they were back in high school again, Steve more handsome than ever, and divorced. All evening they danced and sang to the music of their youth. A hot and heavy three-week romance concluded with their deciding to take the plunge.

Tonight, little did she know that while she slept, a shiny, glowing, metal object was landing in her back yard.

A low frequency hum permeated the yard as the door to the spaceship opened. Maggie's little Scottie, Fido, started barking. When he saw the glowing purple creatures with large, oval-slitted eyes, he ran out into the nearby cornfield and hid. The creatures marched down the ramp of the ship and headed for the house.

Meanwhile, Maggie was dreaming about being at her high school prom, dreaming that Steve had found her in a compromising position with his best friend, Mark. Her dream turned into a nightmare as Mark and Steve laughed, then drove away "together" in a silver Corvette. She began to toss and turn in bed, and woke herself up with a start.

The creatures entered through a screen door that Maggie, in her excitement, had left open. They went into the kitchen and knocked around the pots and pans, opened canisters and tasted everything. They pulled drawers out and ate her dishtowels. They must have really liked them, because little giggly sounds came from them as streams of green goo flew out of tiny openings on their heads, indicating their enjoyment of such a feast. Everything was spilled out or knocked over in the kitchen when they headed for the living room.

Maggie thought she heard something downstairs and called for her dog, Fido. When he didn't come, she struggled to get herself untangled from the blankets, then put on her robe and headed for the stairs. "Fido, what are you into?" she yelled.

The purple creatures stopped and listened to the sound coming from upstairs. They began making squeals and clicks and their large dark eyes swirled with blue lights. They ran around the living room tipping everything in their paths.

Maggie stopped at the top of the stairwell and hollered down to what she thought was her dog. "Fido, what are you doing down there?" She started to head down the stairs after him, when a large crashing sound came from the living room. Intruder, she thought. Maggie ducked back into the hallway, reached into the linen closet and grabbed the plunger. "Who's down there?" she yelled. "I've got a weapon!"

A brilliant purple glow throbbed from the creatures as they heard her, and they formed a circle connecting their long spidery arms. They began to spin and rose up to the ceiling and floated out of the living room and up the stairs. Maggie peeked around the banister and shrieked when she saw the purple glowing creatures heading toward her.

92

"Get out of here. I'm warning you. Get out of my house!" she shouted, pointing the plunger at them. Maggie felt frozen in place. She raised the plunger high over her head, and began flailing it around. "Just try messing with me. I'll knock your little Gumby bodies back to where you came from. You're not fooling with just anyone, you know; I was a star member of St. Mary's softball team! Touch me and I'll splatter you!"

But the spinning purple circle continued to rise up the stairs, stopped over Maggie's head, then dropped down over her, forming a circular vise.

"Help! Help!" she cried out. There was no one around to hear her. "Fido! Fido!" she called over and over, but the dog couldn't hear her out in the cornfield.

She tried whacking them with the plunger, but as the circle tightened around her, she let go of it, and it bonged down the stairs. When they started to spin, Maggie grew dizzy, and passed out. When she awoke she was looking out of a window, the planet Earth getting smaller and smaller. She tried to get up but was strapped to a gurney, pulsating lights and humming sounds all around her. She turned her head and saw the purple creatures.

"You dirty bastards, take me back! I'm getting married tomorrow! I've waited 20 years for a second chance, and an alien abduction won't stop me!" Maggie twisted and turned trying to free herself.

The purple creatures blinked and clicked, but ignored her. She watched as they reached into a large cylinder and pulled out dishtowels with roosters and pigs on them, and shoved them into their gaping mouths, green goo spitting out of their heads.

"Hey!" she yelled, "those are *my dishtowels!*"

By the next day, her little black Scottie, Fido, had returned to the house. He listened as the phone rang and rang all day, his mistress' wedding day.

Five miles across town, Steve pulled the boutonniere from his lapel and threw it down on the church steps. "She got her revenge," he lamented to his best man, Tony.

"Whadaya mean, revenge?" asked Tony, taking off his tuxedo jacket, sitting down on the steps next to Steve, a puzzled look on his face.

"I left her waiting at city hall, right after graduation. I got cold feet – left her standing there. She waited five hours for me to show up. I tried all summer to get back with her, but she said she could never trust a guy who bolted at the last minute. Now, she's had her revenge. She had to wait 20 years, but she really made a jerk out of me." He sighed. "Let's go, Tony. Maybe I can smooth things over, only this time, I'm not taking *no* for an answer."

Alone, tied to the gurney, Maggie cried, knowing Steve had probably left the church, unaware she'd been kidnapped by towel-eating extraterrestrials that poked and prodded her. They even held the end of her own plunger to her nose and pressed and pulled it, watching for her reaction. All she could do was gag, repulsed by the thought of where the circular rubber had been. Then she thought of Fido. Poor little guy, who would care for her precious dog?

Fido waited patiently for Maggie to return, but when she didn't, he sniffed around the kitchen looking for something to eat. His bowl was empty. He went into the pantry where he knew Maggie kept his kibble, but stopped when he noticed green goo gobs on the floor. Being a dog, he went straight over to them and sniffed, then stuck out his big old tongue and lapped them up. Within minutes, Fido felt lightheaded and his vision started to swirl, and when he tried to bark, only odd-sounding squeaks and clicks came out of him. As he staggered out to the back porch, he barely saw the car pulling into the driveway.

Tony and Steve got out of the topaz-colored Jag and walked over to the little dog. "Where's Maggie?" Steve asked Fido, as if he expected the dog to answer.

Before the little Scottie could belch from the green goo, they were inside the house calling his owner.

Maggie, out in space, woke with a start, and there standing over her, was a tall, thin, purple rubber-skinned creature, with large slits for eyes. She stared at him, her eyes wide. He spoke to her in her head. "We are finished with you now. Would you like to return to Earth?" She managed a nod. "Then just tell us where we can get more of your wonderful delicacies."

"What are you talking about?" Maggie demanded

The creature reached into a slot and pulled what was left of her brand new, bridal shower, kitchen towels.

"Book me on the first flight home, and I'll show you where to get enough for your entire planet," she chuckled.

When Steve and Tony searched her house, they found her car in the garage and her purse still hanging in the hall closet, so they called the police. No one noticed that Fido was rolling in the grass out back, glowing purple.

Maggie watched out the ship's window as the planet Earth appeared larger and larger. Soon they were passing through clouds, and trees became visible. In no time flat they were right outside of her town.

"Over there," she pointed to the *Bed Bath & Beyond* store in the mall. "There's where you'll find all the 'delicacies' you could ever want, in every color. But I demand you take me home first."

The ship spun over the mall and headed toward the country, and soon Maggie's farm was in sight. Her heart skipped a beat when she saw Steve's car in her driveway. But she got scared when she saw a police car heading down the road to her house, flashing its lights. Then she looked out to the cornfield and saw her little Fido spinning in the air, glowing purple, his eyes blinking blue.

The creatures took note of Fido, too, and immediately flew their ship to the far end of the field over to the little dog. They quietly landed their saucer, and when they opened the door, Fido ran right up the ramp and into the arms of the tall purple creature. The creature pointed at her, then at the door. "*Go*," she heard him say in her head. "Not without Fido," she said, attempting to grab her dog.

From out of nowhere a spinning circle of creatures seized her again in a vise and took her out of the ship. They quickly dropped her in a cornrow and returned to their saucer. The next thing she saw was Fido looking at her from the ship's window. She thought she saw him chewing on something – a red dish rag – and was certain when she saw green goo splattering the window as the ship disappeared from view.

Steve, Tony, and the police heard her screaming. They rushed out of the house and ran out into the field to find her looking up at the sky, yelling, "Bring my dog back, you bastards!"

No one believed her when she said towel-eating aliens had kidnapped her and stolen her dog. Steve was certain she'd gone crackers, and told her so, adding he was glad he found out before they got married.

With that, Maggie wrote him off and became a woman on a mission. She had to go all the way to Kentland to find towels – seems there weren't any to be had in her town. The local merchants at *Bed, Bath & Beyond, Linens 'N Things,* and *Fieldcrest Outlet* were all briefly hospitalized and placed under heavy sedation when they began telling police that little purple creatures had come into their stores stealing their towels and dish cloths and threatening them with a plunger – then fleeing in a silver saucer. "Mass hysteria," the police called it, started by the woman who'd left her fiancée at the altar.

Maggie loaded her car with every kind of towel she could find. And for months now, night after night, she sits out on her front lawn waving those towels up at the sky, hoping for the return of little Fido.

95

exits/entrances
juley harvey

he died
the day after i met you –
a window closes, a stage door opens,
a spirit flies.
not that it means anything
profound or that i mind –
exactly, it had been so long,
and he, unknowing, without a mind –
but lost is lost,
found is here,
there is a time
once upon,
forever gone.
forever kind.
love's face in the mirror
writes in foggy whispers, blind,
but does not disappear,
molecules merely rearrange
to fit circumstances
that fade, fuse, change.
for the entrances, exits,
for the love, we applaud and cheer.
good-bye, and hello, forever,
my dear.

Valentine's Day
Nancy J. Heggem

On a day such as this, one should review affairs of the heart.
In three score years, I've had a few. When your breath comes in short
strokes and your mind turns one thought over and over.

Ah the 50s, the birth of Rock & Roll. The beat was strong and my
blood ran hot. You were my muscle man, loud and fast.
Yes, first loves are meant to remember, but not to last.

In the 60s, you roared into Chicago.
A new breed, something for Friday nights and hot lights.
Just enough of a line to make you respectable, but too hot for Summer.

The British came: the Beatles, the Avengers, and of course Bond, James
Bond. I had my own English Gentleman, sleek and polished.
We traveled the back roads to country Inns on sun-dappled days.

On to the 70s, the signs of *PEACE*, and I wore flowers in my hair.
You were small and oh so clean and humble –
Laughed at the stuffy folks, stroked guitars and sang folksongs.

Then the 80s came and things got tough, with work to be done.
You knew how to turn work into adventures,
off the beaten track in winter or sun.

Finally the day came: I needed room, more respectability; be serious,
you're getting old. It was time to make the big scary move. But I fell in
love again, with a very respectable silver-maned Ford Taurus.

Good-bye, my loves:
'51 Mercury, '65 Mustang, '67 Austin Healy, '74 VW Beetle,
'79 Chocolate Bunny (Brown VW-Rabbit), and '85 Nissan Truck.
On a really hot day, I crank the AC, pop a CD, cruise I-294 in comfort.

Macintosh Road
Linda Heilscher

acie wondered what she'd been thinking to turn down this road. The sky to the north was overcast, yet here the sun still glowed on the rich autumn foliage making a stunning contrast. She needed to turn around, but something other than her common sense drove the gentle curves. The road would end at a country stand sheltered beneath ancient maples, sentinels to the acres of orchards beyond. For many this road was the highlight of the season: for her it was only a dead end from the past. Earlier in the day, the scent of ripe apples in the air had sparked an unbidden memory that had pierced her. So sharp was the image, it cut through the deadbolt she had placed on her heart so many seasons ago. Now she found herself traveling a road she had sworn she would not venture down again.

How long had it been since she and Nathaniel had last spoken in soft sighs of regret? Two years? Three? Lacie couldn't remember; their coming together and coming apart had blended into a haze of confusing patterns. Their relationship had been good, but doubts and fears had grown to monsters neither one of them had been ready to face, and in the end, love had worn thin until it unraveled. She sighed and shook her head. There was every reason in the world to turn off this road and every reason not to. No other man had been able to fill the shadows he had left behind.

With a determined set to her jaw, Lacie pushed her foot to the pedal, eager to be finished with this foolishness. She had no idea if he was still there in his little country stand at the end of this eternally long road. Perhaps he'd sold the orchard and moved on. Perhaps *his* memories did not awake with the simple scent of apples; perhaps *he* had found another to fill the empty space.

Even now, that crisp autumn day remained vivid in her mind, that day spent in laughter from the mere joy of their togetherness. All had been right with the world then. Sticky and dirty from a morning of apple picking in the orchard, they'd raked the maple leaves, and then thrown themselves in the tall pile. The leaves had all scattered and flattened in their riotous wrestling and gentle loving. She could see his eyes, a soft gray sparkling with merriment, and the scent of apple heavy on his hands as he cupped her face, whispering the words she so longed to hear. Those words had changed everything.

Lacie shook away the memory and glanced at the cloudy sky in the distance, seeing in it the gray of his eyes darkening to thunderheads with anger. The storms between them never lasted, and always they found a resolution that suited them both, even in the end. They hadn't parted in anger or love lost, only in soft regret. The taint of their own personal demons had been too strong and the gamble of commitment too great. This road would bring bittersweet sorrow, ablaze with tiny yellow and orange berries growing along the shoulder. What the hell was she doing?

The last curve gave way and ahead, the weathered cedar display tables stood nestled within the great canopy of golden sugar maples. As always this time of year, the gravel lot was filled with cars and families browsing the bushel baskets of fresh-picked fruit. Children ran helter-skelter among scarecrows, jack-o-lanterns and mazes of hay bales. Lacie's car coasted, her foot itching to hit the brake. This was pure madness.

Nathaniel would be inside bustling about, or on the rickety wooden stool, chewing on his unlit pipe, listening closely to some tale, and overseeing all with a satisfied tilt to his head – just the way she had first seen him on the fateful day that had forever jolted her life. The displays grew closer, but she grew no nearer to knowing what to do.

Lacie's heartbeat quickened; she had come too far and much too close. With all the traffic coming and going, she would have to turn around in the lot. She'd be OK – he wouldn't recognize her since it had been at least two years since they'd seen one another and besides, she had a different car, a different look. Now she wore her chestnut hair in a stylish bob, and gold wire rim glasses graced her face. The rusted pickup had been replaced by a sleek sedan.

With a deep breath, she pulled into the crowded lot and maneuvered beside a large silver van to back out and head for the safety of home. Suddenly, the van doors burst open and a gaggle of children spilled forth. Lacie waited patiently for the mothers to round them up. Checking her mirrors, she reached down to put the car in reverse when a sun warmed hand touched her shoulder through the open window. She stilled, closing her eyes, her breath lost, and sensations she knew so well rushed along her skin.

"Lacie," he said with a soft sigh.

She stiffened and, forcing a nervous smile, looked up into his eyes. "Nathaniel, how are you?"

"Been good," he replied, bending closer. "Won't you come inside for a cup of cider?"

She took in his face, noting new creases around his eyes, and the dark stubble of a long day on his strong jaw. "I'd love to, but I have to head back. I just took a drive to see the colors. You know this road is the best around."

"I'm glad you came this far," he said, lifting his hand from her. "I've missed you, Lacie. I can't pick the Macintosh without thinking about you. Please come in, just for a cup of cider and little catching up."

Her insides fluttered at his mention of the very memory that drove her here. Those days had once held such promise. She heard his name being called and knew he would be gone if she didn't reach out. The reaching out was as hard as the letting go. He turned from her and yelled over his shoulder. The autumn breeze brought the scent of apple from his hand resting on the panel.

"We can't hold it together, Nathaniel, we've tried," Lacie blurted out, feeling an embarrassed flush warm her face.

"Maybe we need to move past the trying," he said, keeping his gaze steady on hers. "To be real honest here, there are things I'd like to say. First off, I haven't been able to move past wanting to be with you, Lacie. I thought I learned that too late, until I saw you pull in. Please stay and hear me out."

Lacie's reply caught in her throat. She knew it was too late. The moment she had felt his touch, it had been too late. An impatient voice called his name again and she forced her way through the anxiety, seeing it for what it was. Their fears had kept them apart, fears they had learned from other relationships, illusions of old torments that had held no place between them. The overcast sky now blocked the sun and muted the bright colors surrounding them, just as the past had dimmed their future.

His deep voice cut the silence. "It's a long road. You could have turned around before you got here."

Lacie heard the hard edge of hurt pride in his tone masking disappointment. Nathaniel had taken a huge risk to say how he felt – not knowing why she had come, or how she would respond. Could she do the same? She gazed into the distance of the crisp autumn day and listened to the leaves rustling across the ground. Rising above it all was the scent of fresh-picked apples. She could no longer deny the truth. It was her heart that had taken this winding road to bring her home again.

"I guess," Lacie admitted, "there isn't a road long enough to keep me away."

Lacie turned off the ignition and saw his smile, and the hope that came with it, grow across his face. It was as though the sun had broken through the gathering clouds and shone for her and her alone. Stepping out of the car, she gave him her hand. Together they walked across the gravel lot and through the door, leaving behind the curious stares and children's laughter to harvest the fruit they'd planted in seasons gone by.

A Mourning Side of Midnight
from *Boys of a Dusky Hue*
Herb Jackson

Chicago's streets were sound asleep as the midnight heat fueled Jazzy's thoughts of fire – the raging fire that had consumed her momma, sister and the Alabama home she'd forsaken years ago, running away with her first love.

She wondered why God had used a fire to make a mother out of her – and why now? Softly singing Billie Holiday's *God Bless the Child*, she pondered this, checking her sleeping nephews.

Afterwards, she sat for hours at her living room window gazing at full moon shadows lurking around gray stone apartment buildings. *Can I be Jazzy the jazz singer and a mother to these boys?* She swallowed shots of gin to rinse the taste and consequences of the ashes of the dead that clogged her throat.

She'd been told their bodies were charred beyond recognition, burnt like useless logs in a smoldering fireplace. From that fire, she inherited her sister's fatherless, eight-year-old twins who'd escaped the blaze but not the nightmares.

The city buildings now appeared as monstrous tombstones, so she moved away from the window. She was hungry, and her mouth felt filthy.

She showered, rinsed her hair, and glared into the mirror, trying to find the face men called irresistible. Gargling cool water she realized she'd killed a few more shots of gin than she'd intended. She gripped the sink, and looked into eyes that had not seen her family in years, hurt because she'd lost any chance to resolve things with her mother.

Just as she knotted the sash on her yellow, satiny robe, she heard the metal of Willie's key twisting the lock. She believed she would always have them both – her first love and Willie. For a while, she did. But after she'd brought Little Sissy's orphaned kids home, Willie refused to let her love them. Hated her caressing them – shut down her capacity to love him. Tonight she mourned her loss of love with shots of gin and tears.

Sweet Willie climbed the stairs, wasted, hoping Jazzy was asleep, but she was out of the bathroom and at him as he pulled the front door shut.

They stood inches apart at the door, separated only by the humid night heat trapped in the apartment. Willie reeked of lilacs and licorice, some other woman's whorish odor. For the longest minute, their eyes locked in a noiseless duel, hers fiery and furious, his distant and cold.

She found herself floating in Willie's deep dark face, following his fingers as they combed through his slicked waves of graying hair. *The blacker the berry, the sweeter the juice,* her mother said. That's why Jazzy called him Sweet Willie. Her father had been a dark man, a sweet man.

Three years ago, after many other men, Willie had conjured up in her the image of her father, a man of calm, and calmness; the kind of calm you felt on a sun bright day – the kind Sweet Willie had brought back into her life. Lately though, he had erupted into a mountain of rage with no trace of the Willie who'd drawn her to him.

This new Willie blocked the sunshine from her life.

As a young girl, she would often escape Alabama's summer heat to scan the sun's peaceful reflection on the surface of the Chattahoochee River. Full of song, smells of sweet honeysuckle and moist earth, she would belt out gospels, blues melodies, or jazz rhapsodies only the birds could hear.

Her father always wanted his coffee cream-colored light and loaded down with sugar. Taking his first sip each morning, he would wink at her with a big-faced grin that illuminated his coal black face and repeat his favorite line: *"Like my coffee jist like my women! Sweeter than sorghum and bright as sunlight!"* One morning he finished his sweet coffee, stood up and stretched his massive arms high over his head, then fell on the kitchen floor asleep, never to wake again.

On that day of mourning, she wanted to swim out and climb atop the sun's reflection when some meddlesome clutter became clear in her mind; the words SUN-shine, SUN-light, SUN-day – made her think happy thoughts – then she realized that within her soul all the brightness of the sun was dying, cremated by its own fires.

She was at the burial when she figured out she loved something more than her father – her music, and it would die inside her if she stayed in Alabama any longer. So, at seventeen and without a word to a living soul, Jazzy jetted with her music to Chicago. Her mother never forgave her.

◈

Purring or belting songs into Chicago microphones took the edge off the strangeness of the big city. Her music protected her, held her up, and caressed her until perspiration drooped her hairdo away, and her vocal cords strained to inflammation. She could never get enough – she would sing and sing with her mouth stretched wide declaring her faithfulness to the music she loved.

For the past few months, though, she feared she was losing her love; not Willie, but her music. She struggled to express this to him, but Willie stood at the doorway and spoke first. "Me or them. Me or them, Jazzy. Just like I said yesterday. "

She swallowed hard. "Dammit, Sweet, these are my sister's kids. You want me to kick 'em out when I'm all they got?"

Finally, the big man blinked and took in a deep breath that expanded his huge chest until his camel hair coat spread wide enough to reveal his nipples pressing against his silk shirt. He spoke with his massive hand pushed to his forehead.

"All right. All right now...back off, Jazzy. I ain't in the mood for no crap tonight. 'Specially with them little country-butt boys here. I told you to take them to the welfare people, but naw – you got to let them stay and screw everything up."

She pounced on the word 'crap' repeating it louder than she expected. "Crap! That's what I'm talking about! All this *crap* you been laying on me for the last couple of months has got to stop!" Jazzy heard herself say "all sis scrap" instead of "all this crap."

Willie shook his head in disgust and moved a couple of quick steps around her and into the darkness of the front room.

Momma and Sissy gone in a fire...now with all this weight, she thought. *Willie, you selfish pig, you don't deserve me...*

With that, she pushed him in the back with both hands. "Dammit, don't walk away!"

Willie sat on the arm of the couch and folded his arms, yelling, "You better not be trying to cop an attitude!"

The force of Willie's voice staggered her. Light-headed and barefoot she thought of the boys and tapped a nervous finger to her lips, "Shhhh, Sweets, let's don't wake up the boys!" Her tongue slurred so it came out, *dwake-up-be-toys.*

She sensed a familiar storm about to crash around them, so tried to quiet Willie's lightning quick temper by coming on sexy. She touched the back of his hand. Slipping loose the sash on her robe she commanded herself, *I will win him over. I can make it all right.* After all, she had spent years with Willie and knew the best way to handle him.

She didn't want to leave him, but unless he did the right thing by the boys...

She started a slow, awkward, gyration of her hips. Arms crossed, Willie watched unsmiling until her robe draped open enough to expose a hint of her tight stomach and naked thighs. The lamp in the bedroom set her creamy complexion aglow. Willie's lips forced a smile into the eyes he called beautiful.

"C'mon, you know I love you, Sweets." Her eyelids fluttered on each syllable, but her slurring tongue said, "*Tweets*." She giggled at herself, then wished she hadn't finished off the whole pint of gin.

Seeing how juiced she was, Willie tired of her come-on. A full head taller, he jumped to his feet, flexed his back, and tossed his camel hair jacket behind him. Without missing a beat his nostrils flared and he gave her a red-eyed chuckle, then cracked smooth on her.

"What you babbling about? You love me? Look, I done told you, it ain't no in-between with me, you dig?" Stepping out of his Florsheims and unbuckling his belt, he pulled his pants off letting his voice grow fiercer with each piece of clothing he shed.

"Just like you can't eat caviar and pigs' feet! You can't be my woman and some welfare mama! I'm telling you for the last time. It's me or them!"

Jazzy fingered her lips and pulled her robe closed. Willie discarded his silk tie at her feet.

Mean, she thought. Cold. Cold enough to freeze the nuts off a brass *monkey*. Every day he got colder and crueler; she had lost him; whatever they once had was broken, gone, lost. Willie upped the ante with her most secret regret. "...And don't start handing me all that banana and cream BS about your dead mama. When was the last time you set eyes on her, 12 years ago?"

It didn't matter it was true; it hurt like he wanted. He used to be crazy about me, she thought. Used to chew on my shoulders, suck on my toes. I used to serenade him to sleep. A country saying sprang from memory: *Drink hard and shack up with strangers, you'll be lying dead in a flashy casket by 30.* She had just turned 29.

At that thought she narrowed her eyes and hissed, "To hell with you! Coming on like some phony street pimp! Talking 'bout *I loves you, Jazzy! Do any-thang for you, Jazzy*. Telling me we going to the stars together – well, Mr. Big-time promoter, ain't you the one making *your* money offa *my* singing? And yeah, I fixed up that back room for the kids. Yeah, I got 'em in school." Her eyes swept past him and rested on the bedroom mirror, where she played to her reflection.

"Yeah, it does feel good to be acting like a mother to them boys, 'cause they need me! And one more thing! 'Less you change your attitude I want your dirt-black behind outta here tomorrow and I ain't joking!"

It was more than she wanted to say, and it hit him hard. Willie stood in front of her wearing only his shorts; he widened his stance pointing his fingers at her thumb up, like a gun, just inches from her nose. The spit flying behind his words sprayed her forehead. "Now you dig it, Jazzy! All the men you been screwing around with, and you want Sweet Willie to turn square and set up house! You is, *gots* to be kidding! Until them little bastards showed up, we was swinging along real good. Getting our kicks and making dough! Now, just when the dice is rolling good, and we got a chance to get on the road and move into the big-time, on the white side of the tracks, all I'm hearing is you can't sing diddly-squat 'cause you spending nights here – with them!"

Willie rolled his big shoulders and put a deep roll in his voice. "Maybe Chicago is too much for you. Maybe you oughta climb your yella-rump back on a bus back down to Alabama, and get to singing in one of them honky-tonk juke joints!"

Jazzy's thoughts raced to her nephews sleeping in the back, so she moved in close to cup Willie's mouth and kiss him quiet. He grabbed her wrist and her nails raked the softness of his cheek. She didn't mean to scratch his face. He shoved her away then pulled her back to him by her robe. His hand reached high and slapped Jazzy so hard her knees buckled. She touched the stinging place on her mouth, her lips wet with blood, then slapped him back. Which usually ended their confrontations, but this time like an echo, she felt the sting and weight of Willie's hand on her face. She countered with a blow to his jaw. It didn't faze him. He slapped her again, and again, open hand, backhand, left cheek, right cheek, back and forth until her face burned scalding hot, and she collapsed to the floor.

He kneeled down next to her and tore at her robe. Exhausted, she could feel the brush of his fingertips rake through her hair as the smell of the other woman's heavy perfume filled her mouth. Bumping heads, she struggled against his heavy hands pressed down on her shoulders. He was too strong. His mouth sucked the breath from her lips. She let him plunge his enormous stiffness deep into the only softness left for him, but not deep enough to remove her desire to leave him.

He was a rock blocking her sunshine. She was a bird cringing under his weight. Her fingers clawed the rock, scraping the flesh of Willie's back. The strength of her thighs balanced his heaviness.

Stretched flat on the floor with her ankles twined around his calves, she began to rock and roll.

Tonight is only for the boys, only for the boys... She thought over and over until Willie groaned loose his current of violence.

Jazzy was so dazed she closed her wings around him so she wouldn't fall off the floor, but now at least she knew she could fly away on the wings of her first love. Because she couldn't trust Willie with her love again.

She felt Willie's heartbeat pounding against the softness of her breast. His cheek rubbed the side of her face. He blew a labored breath into her ear saying, "That's all you needed, baby." Jazzy wedged her hands against his chest and pushed him off. Willie let himself roll onto his back. After a little while, his breathing slowed and he dozed off. She squeezed her eyes full of tears and thought of sunshine.

When she got to her feet, her first thought was to varnish Willie's face with hot grits, or slice his throat with a butcher knife. Instead, she flew away in the night with her sister's kids in tow. Running from him. Back to her first love – the music she vowed never to leave again. Willie was right. Maybe Chicago was too much for her and the boys. But her first love would take care of them wherever they landed.

Canvas
Grace Papelera Kavanaugh

"Restructure" meant – try a different dance.
Wipe the canvas white. Sketch what I desire.
Must draw, must paint, though I'm still in a trance.
Calm my bitter heart – peel off the barbed wire.

New hopes. New fears. Refine my other dreams.
Only to erase, spreading shades of gray.
My brush twirls and dips, mixing color schemes.
Paint the canvas. Breathe. Visualize Monet.

The sea – a turquoise blanket by the shore.
Magnify each detail, blend, be exact.
Water lilies blush like an open sore.
For beauty captivates, stain and distract.

To wait, to love and grow with my shadow.
Swirling in this canvas is *ME!* Hello.

11○

My Daughter, My Love
Marie Loggia-Kee

ove and loss come in many forms. There's the love of a romantic partner and the love of a child. There's the loss of a parent and sometimes, horrifically, the loss of a child. Those youngest, most vulnerable, often result in the most tragic losses. This is a story of love, loss, and love the second time around.

The Loss: Some small dark clumps clung to the bottom of the toilet bowl. A nightlight illuminated the room. In the middle of the night, the whirl of the fan and glare of fluorescents overpowered my senses. I'd been waking up in the middle of the night to pee more often. Even in the shadows, I knew that what had come out of me wasn't just urine. Please, God, no. Not this. Not now. Not me.

I turned on the light, eyes blinking in the brightness, looked at the toilet and saw red. Red streaks floating through the red, and not making orange. I'd been having cramps and some spotting the past 24 hours, hips propped up over pillows and bed-ridden, but nothing like this. I used to welcome the blood, the giver of life. Not this time. This time, it meant death.

The cold plastic clunked in my hand as I lifted the seat up. The doctor's words echoed in my head: "If you pass anything, try to collect it so we can test it." In there. In those blood clots, could be my baby and I needed to dig it out.

I knelt by the side, tears splashing off the rim. Only days ago I was throwing up. Now, look at me. I stuck my hand into tepid water, through the prenatal-vitamin-stained urine and felt around in the bottom of the bowl. I grabbed a few clots, their murky textures slipping through my fingers and pulled up. My fingers rubbed together, feeling for what? I was only six weeks pregnant. How was I supposed to find something the size of a pencil eraser or smaller in this? Blood streamed through my fingers back into the bowl, a drop splashing on the porcelain. I'd have to clean that up, too. I dipped my hand back in, and felt nothing, nothing but hopelessness. What was alive inside me was gone. I had no proof except for the aloneness that I felt: totally isolated and alone.

Still on my knees, I said a prayer for my loss, a good-bye, took a piece of tissue, wiped the rim and flushed my child away.

—◇—

The Love: Two months after the child I lost would have been born, Cassandra joined our lives.

"How does that feel?" asks my mother as I nurse my daughter.

I say one word, "Magical."

Cassandra's lips wrap around my nipple. Her tongue laps on the lower part of it, drawing the milk out. When the milk lets down, a pins-and-needles sensation flows through my breasts, a feeling similar to when a limb falls asleep and starts to regain feeling. As the milk slows, a tugging sensation takes over, internally near my armpits, as if my daughter is pulling the last of the milk from the ducts. The first few weeks of nursing, Cassie would suckle with her eyes shut, concentrating all her energy upon feeding. Now, eyes wide open, she takes it all in. I often look down at her, and ask her what she's doing and her lips turn up in a playful smile around my dark brown areola. It's become a game for her and less of a chore for me.

112

Mornings, I wake with a fog clouding my brain. It's as if my head was lost in San Francisco Bay's most overcast day and I cannot find my way. But, it's not from imbibing too many Raspberry Margaritas, sneaky Cosmos or full-bodied glasses of Chianti. Oh, how I wish. Rather, it's from not enough partaking of shut-eye.

Cassandra usually wakes me before 6:30 A.M. I hear her movement over the baby monitor, stumble out of bed, use the bathroom and go into her room. While she's always awake before me, I never wake to her crying. She patiently waits until I enter the room, and then I'm flashed with a smile that clearly explains how happy she is to see me.

After I change her soggy diaper, we climb into my bed, where I feed her lying down and, if I'm lucky, we fall back to sleep. Some days, we sleep until 9 A.M. Other mornings, at 7:30, I feel her legs and arms kicking and stretching for attention. If I try to ignore her action, she'll caress my face with her chubby fingers.

At night, she falls asleep before 10 P.M. If I would only go to bed at the same time, I wouldn't be using cover-up on the lavender rings under my eyes. Instead, I stay awake until 2 A.M. For it's the nighttime, after Cassie and my husband go to sleep, that I get my time alone.

As an only child, I'm used to alone time. As a mother, my alone time doesn't happen much. All the clichés ring true. My life is no longer my life. My body is no longer my body. Cassie haunts my thoughts while I teach in front of the classroom, while shopping, in bed. My husband and I rarely get to spend time together; sometimes, it's as if we're two single parents living together.

In the end, that one morning smile makes everything else worthwhile.

The subject of miscarriage continues to remain taboo. Many do not want to acknowledge the love and loss of an unborn child. Friends and family shy away from the subject. When I try to talk to my husband, he says it makes him feel – too sad. How can a person love something that is unknown? A mother does. The only person who listens, hugs and cries with me, is my mother.

People ask me if we plan on having a second child. To be honest, I often feel as if there is a little boy, waiting to join our lives. I don't know if this is the spirit of the one that we lost, or one that's still to come.

Every September, I privately mourn the child that I lost, the one that graced our lives for a few short weeks, and every November, we celebrate our daughter's birth. Yet, life teaches that there's many different types of love. The loss of one love often brings another. If I had been unable to live with the loss of my first pregnancy, I would have been too afraid to try again, and never would have known my current love. For love – the second time around – is ever so poignant and graceful.

114

Snowblind
Austin Kelly

t never snows, she thought. The wind blows, the drifts pile and the air mists before your face as you exhale in the bitter chill, but... It never snows anymore.

Zella stared out across the barren field of white which went on forever as the morning sun reflected brilliantly across the flickering ice crystals that blew over the drifts. She tightened the coarsely woven scarf around her neck, trying to keep out more of the wind that fought tenaciously to nip at any flesh even miminally exposed.

"Zell? Zell, are ya packed?" called a voice from behind her.

She turned to see Christi leaning her head out the door of the old power station they had slept in the last few nights. Christi's luxuriant brown hair billowed around her head in the wind. Her knit sweater was tattered, but it lent her more character than criticism.

"I'll be right in!" she said, and watched as Christi withdrew inside.

Resuming her reflection, Zella cast her gaze back upon the white nothingness that stretched as far as she could see. It wasn't always like this. There were cities, fields, roads – and people everywhere. And there was warmth. Before the WhiteFall.

She walked back to the building, which was half buried in the dozen feet of snow that was now frozen solid across the ground. It had taken them nearly a day to dig out enough room in the snow to get the door open, and another day to sweep up enough of the dust and grime off the floor to make sleeping space. It was unfortunate they were having to leave so soon, but they had to keep moving.

Pulling open the heavy, stiff door, Zella entered the cavernous space of the old power station with huge generators lining the walls and the thick power cables that snaked their way in and out of other giant pieces of equipment that had not functioned in months. The sound of her boots being stomped on the concrete to knock off the snow echoed through the expanse.

"Zella, hurry and help Brian pack these towels he found."

Finishing with her boots, Zella peered between two of the generators, where she could see Jesse working awkwardly with several stacks of bath towels. She liked him. Maybe it was more than that. He was feisty, cocky, and cute in a thin, shaggy rock star way. His brilliant blue eyes often defied whatever dull pain he was always hiding as they stared lamentingly through his floppy, chin-length hair.

"Okay, Jesse," she said as she removed her scarf and hat, revealing short black hair. She brushed snow off the arms of her heavy wool coat, and then removed it, hanging it next to the three others on nails near the door.

She walked around the iron beams that mounted one of the generators to its base. There, Jesse was bent over, trying to lift an awkward stack of the terrycloth and place it in a duffel bag. She paused, admiring his tight ass and slim waist. When she realized she was staring, she quickly went to his side, helping him steady the pile.

"Thanks, Zell," he said, smiling at her with a warmth she often thought could heat the world. Maybe it had once. Long ago.

He zipped the bag, and hefted it onto his shoulder. "Brian's downstairs. He's gonna stay here a few hours, finish covering our tracks and catch up beyond the next drift. He wants us to set up camp there."

Zella scrunched her brow, as she often did when Brian played the overprotective leader.

"How long?"

"He'll be at camp by dark."

She nodded. It was common for Brian to stay behind and cover their tracks. There were dozens of other nomadic groups wandering across the frosty terrain, and many would do anything to get food or warmer clothing. It still made her nervous. Brian was fun, goofy. He was also an important part of the glue that kept them together.

Christi stepped up behind them. "Let's move."

⸺◇⸺

They had made it over the first drift faster than they had thought, across its crust so thickly frozen that they could walk carefully on its surface for quite a distance. Finding the remnants of an old gas station, they made camp. The snow was high enough that only the top of the remaining rain canopy over the pumps was visible. Christi, always the smart one, suggested they dig camp underneath the steel roof, and over the next three hours, they did.

As usual, Christi had her camp set first, and began to scout the area. It was as much for their protection as for her own curiosity. Zella always liked these times the most, as it left her alone with Jesse.

She finished propping the final post on her thermal tent, and lay down in her thick, warm blankets, still wearing her winter coat. It was always better when they had an actual building that would hold some heat, but most times it was more like this. Looking across the dimly lit cave they had dug, she could see Jesse sitting upright in his own tent, his wool trench coat wrapped around his body.

"Could be colder," she observed.

He looked to her, and smiled out of the right half of his mouth. "I was thinkin' about putting on swim trunks."

Letting out a small laugh, she rolled onto her stomach, propping her head up on her forearms. "I miss that. Pools. Beaches. Not as much as cupcakes, but a lot..."

Jesse smiled at her again, and turned back into his tent, digging around in one of his satchels. He was always so difficult to get talking. It seemed to Zella if he had his way, he'd just never talk. But there was also something there that demanded being social.

This was the mystery that attracted her to him. Everyone always talked about life before the WhiteFall. Campfire reminiscing about life before the WeatherCore Project went all to hell was common among the nomads. Zella had been only 17 when the environmentalists destroyed the WeatherCore Project, and she imagined Jesse couldn't have been much older. He might have been in college, though he never said, and she longed to find out.

Zella crawled out of her tent and across the hard ice to the mouth of his tent, kneeling just inside.

Turning to look at her, he shoved the gear in his hand back into the bag he had pulled it from.

"What?" he asked, with just a hint of arrogance.

"Where were you?"

Dropping into a sitting position, he rested his arm on his bent knee, and scrunched his eyebrows at her. "Where was I when?"

She settled, subtly blocking the exit to his tent. In the back of her mind, she wondered if she cornered him because she was curious, or was the metaphor more sexual?

"The first night of the WhiteFall."

He fidgeted in a sort of squirrel-ly reaction.

"A, uh... A dorm. In Utah. I was in college."

She nodded. One of the three North American WeatherCore berths had been in Utah. The other two were on either coast. "You must've gotten snow almost immediately."

"You?"

"Senior Prom."

He laughed, a cocky laugh that was accentuated by rolling his eyes at her.

"What? It isn't funny!" she retorted, starting to giggle.

The two of them sat there, smiling in the cold for several moments, before Zella began absently playing with a button on her coat.

"Bobby Gorman. He borrowed his mom's car to take me. He was kinda a yearbook dork."

Jesse snickered.

"I'm serious," she answered, smiling, her slightly raspy voice squeaking. "He was cute. I thought he was cute, anyway. He bought me a corsage, a little carnation thing probably from a grocery store..."

Again, Jesse smiled at her. She looked up and met his eyes, and felt not so cold.

"Okay, he was kind of a geek. Were you?" he asked, biting his bottom lip.

"Little bit." She tossed a fold of her coat into her lap for warmth. "He was my first love. There's nothing like that, ya know? Like, the sweaty hands when we danced, the smell of the cheap cologne he used too much of to impress me. We were in the backseat of his mom's car behind the Dairy Blend when the first snow started." She sighed, "He was my first..."

"You don't ever replace that," he answered. "Every time later it's just... different."

Pausing, she rolled her eyes and chuckled. "There haven't been any other times."

"What happened?"

"I don't know," she said, her voice husky with curiosity and hesitance. "You remember that first week of snow. The panic. The chaos. Everyone sorta hunkered down and held on tight, not really sure what was happening. I mean, it was the middle of May and snowing everywhere."

Jesse lowered his eyes, hiding the pain of WhiteFall memories. She just kept talking, her own pain eased since he seemed to be listening attentively as she continued.

"The news kept talking about the unknown. How...how no one was sure how Mother Nature would react to suddenly being in control of the weather again. Then there was all the military..." She trailed off, remembering the giant tanks thrusting their way through the deep drifts, trying to enforce martial law and maybe keep the highways passable. It was fruitless. In two weeks, it had all become a wasteland, and the snow would continue to fall for another two. People froze, starved and killed each other over wool coats and theology.

The whole world brought to this, she thought, envisioning the white field extending on forever beyond their cover. All of everything for nothing.

Quietly reflecting, she wondered quietly aloud, "Did they ever catch all of the terrorists?"

"No," he answered, almost a whisper.

She stared at him, trying to read his face, its blankness glacial as the planet around them. It should have frustrated her. It should have made her angry, made her pry and push to find out more. Why didn't it?

Zella's brow furrowed as she mulled her feelings.

"What is it?" Jesse asked.

"Nothing."

She crawled further into the tent, closer to him.

Jesse just watched as she moved near, reaching out, and placing her hand on his cheek. Zella stared at him a long moment, and then moved closer. Their lips touched gently, carefully walking across cracked ice. Zella's hand moved from his face to his neck, and onward across his chest, feeling the gentle crevice between his muscles rise and fall with his increasingly rapid breathing.

Suddenly, he pulled away, falling onto his back and holding her up by the shoulders. He looked scared, worry having crept across his face. The heat Zella was feeling between them told her he wanted this, yet he moved away.

Zella slowly pushed his hands off her shoulders, holding herself above him. She would not lose him this close.

"I love you."

His confusion mounted, and he glanced to the side of the tent, and then back at her. By the time his eyes had found hers again, they showed less confusion and more disbelief.

"You can't love me."

Leaning into him, Zella knew what she felt. She ran her hand through his hair, grasping him closer.

"It's my decision," she said as she took his upper lip into her mouth and fervently nipped. For an instant, he was unmoving, and then reciprocated.

As they kissed, her hands roamed his body, slipping his coat off his shoulders and working his shirt over his head. The cold immediately hardened his nipples, and she warmed them with her tongue. He moaned, and she continued there as her hands opened his pants, pushing them downward to reveal more than she had expected.

Just below his waistline, on the taut, left flat of his lowest stomach muscle, was a WeatherCore barcode tattoo. She just stared at it, paralyzed, unsure what to do. Very slowly, he sat up on his elbows, and pulled his boxers up to cover himself.

Terrified, she understood, "You weren't in a dorm room."

He let out a slow sigh.

"Who are you?" she demanded.

Jesse averted his eyes, looking at the tent wall again, not answering.

He looked up at her finally, but his pleading face and unspeaking, open mouth gave no more insight. Zella had never met anyone with the Project. Brian and Christi often debated who was more to blame: the company that egotistically took weather out of the hands of Mother Nature, or the environmentalists who blew up the Project to recklessly give it back. Honestly, Zella had never thought about it before.

Slowly, Jesse reached out and took her hand, leading her back to a kneeling position. "My father was an engineer at the Utah berth. Pretty high up. He got me a job the summer before the WhiteFall in shipping and receiving. It was a nothin' thing."

"Then why keep it secret?"

"People like Brian," he explained. "People blame the Project as much as the terrorists."

"Where's your dad?"

"When we first left Boise, we fell in with a group of nomads from Iowa. My father told them over dinner one night he'd worked for WeatherCore." Trying to avoid his feelings, Jesse began putting his jeans back on. "They didn't take too kindly to it."

"I'm sorry," Zella comforted, reaching out to him.

He nodded, and she lay into his chest, pushing him down and holding him.

Crawling out from the bunker, Zella got to her feet and looked around. She found Jesse a few feet away, watching the morning sun rise over the level snowscape. The sun reflected brilliant orange and red off the expanse of ice, so Jesse lifted a hand to shield his eyes. She moved to his side, squinting, as the wind blew ice crystals across their view.

"My father did this," he said, hushed.

"No one has to know."

Gazing at the smooth plane, it often seemed as though the world had become so flat, one could see all the way across. And even then, there was still more desolation.

"There's no one to tell, Zella."

She looked back to the canopy, and could see in the hole beneath it that Brian and Christi had not returned during the night. Her stomach turned, knowing they were probably dead and imagining their coats and gear on other nomads.

"What do we do now?" she asked, the sun warm on her face.

"We drift."

A Story of Jamestown (excerpt)
K. B. Laugheed

A pril 14, 1610: Last August, over 600 English men, women and children settled in this new colony of Jamestown, Virginia. Now only 50 of us have survived these first months here – so many lost in less than a year...

⬥

Thomas had not been alone with Sarah for...well, for years, actually. Since before Tom was born. But now he found himself walking beside this woman who was his wife, and for once there were no other human beings in sight. It was a little awkward, a little frightening, a little exciting.

The children were at the stream upriver where William and his pals were constructing a fish weir. Sarah and Thomas had gone with them and watched as they set up the stick walls, but when it was apparent this project would take hours, Sarah wanted to collect greens to cook with the fish. Thomas went with her, carrying a smoldering musket.

He was getting used to carrying a gun. Twice in the last two weeks, he'd fired it – once accidentally when shifting it from hand to hand, and once when he shot wildly at a darting rabbit. He'd missed the rabbit by a wide margin, of course, but the attempt had given him a bit of a thrill. Lately he was even starting to enjoy the way the gun felt in his hands. It gave him a sense of control and made him feel like a man – a real man – instead of a simpering victim of circumstance.

Today, however, he needed no gun to feel good about himself. The day was perfect. Flowers were wafting up great waves of heady perfume, the birds were singing, fighting, mating, or doing all three at once, and the air was so warm that for the first time in months Thomas had left his house wearing only breeches and a thin linen shirt. Sarah carried her mobcap, filled with greens. The farther they walked, the more they began to enjoy this rare chance to be alone. They stopped

121

looking for greens and started looking instead at the trees, the birds, the flowers. At one point their shoulders bumped together, and Thomas smiled as he took his wife's hand in his. They had walked hand-in-hand like this years ago when they were kids, sneaking off to a tryst behind the blacksmith's barn. But that tryst was so long ago and so, so far away, in another lifetime, in another world. Thomas stared at the ground and swallowed hard. Suddenly he asked, "Sarah, do you ever wonder why we've survived?"

She inhaled and exhaled slowly. "Deciding who survives and who does not is God's job, not mine, and I'm glad to leave Him to it. I see no point in troubling myself over someone else's business. I'm grateful for this day, Thomas. That's all I know."

"Yes, of course, but still – you have to wonder, don't you? Why us? Were we saved for some specific reason? I didn't want to survive any more than George, Richard, and John. I didn't try harder. I wasn't more suited for it. In many ways, each of them was more suited for survival than I. So why am I the last one standing?"

"You're not exactly the last," Sarah pointed out. "I'm here – and Jane, Anna, and Maud. There's Elizabeth, William, and the other children. You're far from alone, Thomas."

122

He shook his head, unable to put his complicated thoughts into words. After a moment he said, "I'm sorry I made you come here, Sarah. I...I lied to you. I told you we'd be rich, we'd be powerful, we'd have titles and prestige. I told you we'd have land, but we've ended up with nothing – nothing!"

Sarah shrugged. "I never wanted any of those things."

"Then why did you agree to come? What did you want if not those things?"

Sarah wrapped her free hand around Thomas's upper arm to pull him closer to her. "I wanted to be with you."

He was so stunned he could not respond for a time, and he walked blindly, enjoying the feel of her warm, round breast against his arm, her cheek against his shoulder. "I'm an idiot," he said at last. "I've always been an idiot. As I look back on my life, I can't believe what an idiot I've always been. I've been so very, very stupid that I never even had any inkling of how very stupid I was. And to this day every time something happens to show me how stupid I am, I'm always surprised. Every single time. I'm that stupid."

Sarah chuckled. "Well, if you know how stupid you are, then at least you're not as stupid as you used to be! You're making progress!" She poked her husband in his side, making him smile. Before long, they arrived at a clearing where several ravines came together to form a small rainwater pond. It was so picturesque – a bright and shining gem in the dark expanse of the woods – that they sank to the ground, awed by the beauty of the place. "Oh look!" Sarah said as she laid her cap down and leaned over the water. "What are these, Thomas?"

Thomas looked and saw countless tiny, black creatures wriggling about in the water. There were hundreds of them – thousands. Thousands of thousands. He looked along the edge of the pond in both directions, and as far as he could see, those creatures were thick in the shallows. "They're tadpoles!" he exclaimed.

"Tadpoles? You mean baby frogs?" When Sarah diddled her fingers in the water, several hundred of the small fish-like creatures darted away. She laughed and pulled her hand out. Slowly but surely the tadpoles swam back. "Where did they all come from?"

"Mummy and daddy frogs, I'd say," Thomas grinned, and Sarah rolled her eyes.

"No, I mean, were they born here, or washed here by the rain? Surely this pond hasn't been here long."

Thomas shrugged. "Wherever they came from, they're here now. Millions of 'em." He and Sarah watched the tadpoles. Some stayed near the shore while others stayed in deep waters. Some preferred the shade, while others stayed in the sun. Some darted frantically away if a leaf or twig blew down upon the water, while others froze in place and waited for the ripples to subside.

193

"This pond will dry up soon," Sarah murmured. "I wonder what will happen to them then."

"Some will change into frogs, I suppose, and the others, well – they'll be out of luck. Ducks and other things will eat some. Mayhap they'll eat each other. The rest will just die."

"Surely not!" Sarah said, slightly alarmed. "Why would God make so many, just to let most suffer and die?"

"Well, it wouldn't do to have them all make it, would it, Sarah? I mean, if all these tadpoles turned into frogs, the forest would be thick with them! 'Twould be frogs knee deep, from here all the way to the river. 'Twould be a plague of frogs of Biblical proportions! 'Tis just as well only a few survive. Otherwise they'd be all over us."

Sarah giggled as Thomas made his fist hop about on the shore as if it were a frog, bouncing it up her leg and onto her belly, where it attempted to jump into her bodice. She grabbed his fist and, with a devilish grin, pretended to bite it. "I wonder if tadpoles are tasty. George's Mary once told me the French eat frogs."

Thomas smiled ruefully. "I've eaten worse." His eyes glazed over and his face grew somber as he pulled his hand away and turned back to the pond.

Sarah pressed her lips together in a thin line as she looked for some way to restore her husband's lighter mood. She picked up a rock and made as if to throw it. "If you're worried about a plague of frogs, Thomas, we could throw this rock and smash a hundred right now. Most are bound to die anyway – you said so yourself – so what difference would it make? That lot swimming under that log – I'll bet they think they're clever to have found a hiding place! What if I threw my rock there and made short work of all their cleverness? They'd never know what hit them, and the others would thank me for getting them out of their way!"

"Don't, Sarah!" Thomas said sharply. "Leave them be." He took the rock from her slowly, gently, an odd expression in his eyes. "They're just like us, don't you see? They're just like us." He numbly dropped the rock into the weeds and sat staring at the multitudes of tadpoles in the pond. "'Tis nothing we did, is it? 'Tis not because we darted right when the others darted left, or because we hid under a log or didn't hide under a log. 'Tis just because our part of the pond didn't dry up, and no ducks came to eat us, and no crazy woman threw a rock in on us. 'Tis because we somehow managed to eat the others before they had a chance to eat us. We're just like the tadpoles, Sarah. I didn't deserve to live any more than John, George, or Richard did. My survival was not because of anything I did or didn't do. I was just lucky, that's all. Just plain lucky."

Sarah frowned. "What you call luck Reverend Potter would have called the Hand of God. The preachers say God guides your every move, makes you dart right instead of left, helps you avoid the falling rocks, and keeps you in the last bit of pond water before it dries. Why call it luck instead of God's Will?"

"Because Potter..." Thomas paused a moment. "I don't know, Sarah. Calling it God's Will implies such a dreadful obligation. If God has truly saved me for some purpose, then I must fulfill it, but how can I possibly fulfill it if I don't even know what that purpose is?"

"How can you possibly fail to fulfill it? Perhaps your purpose was to be right here right now, to drop that rock so someone else will stumble over it weeks, years or decades from now! You can't know why some things happen, Thomas, any more than one of those tadpoles could know why I might throw a rock!"

"But if it is not given to me to understand, Sarah, then why is it given to me to wonder? It seems a cruel hoax. Does God mock us?"

Sarah shook her head and sighed. "You think too much, Thomas. You take yourself way too seriously. You said we're like tadpoles – do you see any of them sitting around bemoaning their cruel fate? Do you see them brooding or grumbling or demanding answers from God? If you think God mocks us, what of them? A million dead within the month? And that's just here! There are tadpole ponds all over the world, Thomas! Do you honestly hope to understand the reason behind the death of every single living creature, great and small? You? You said it yourself, love – you're just not that smart!"

Thomas looked down at the sun shimmering on the pond water, and all of a sudden he felt overwhelmingly relieved. For some reason, it was incredibly liberating to conclude he did not have to understand why God had kept him alive while so many others had died; a tremendous weight was lifted from his weary shoulders. If, indeed, Thomas had been chosen for some Divine Purpose, apparently he did not need to know what that Purpose was, and, in fact, probably wouldn't understand it even if it was explained to him in excruciating detail. After all, Thomas wasn't very smart. Luckily, being smart didn't seem to count for all that much in the greater scheme of things.

Sarah put her hand on his shoulder; he felt it soft and warm through the thin linen. He leaned over to kiss her mouth, and she kissed his, leaning back in the soft grass with a happy sigh. He lay on top of her, and in a moment they were enjoying each other's bodies in a way they had not enjoyed each other's bodies for many, many months. In fact, they enjoyed each other's bodies in a way they had never enjoyed each other's bodies, for never before had they been so very aware they were alive, and so very, very aware of how easily they might not be.

When it was over, they moaned and sighed and whimpered and smiled. Thomas no longer cared why he had survived while others had not. He cared only that he had survived and was, therefore, able to savor this delicious moment. Lying naked in the sun, he tickled Sarah's breasts with a sprig of grass while she giggled and writhed, telling him to stop tormenting her. To retaliate, she pulled up a handful of grass and was dribbling it across his back when a shadow fell across her face. Thomas saw her go white as she looked over his shoulder, and from the sheer terror in her eyes, he knew what she was looking at even before he turned to see. When he did turn, he saw four savages staring down at them. One of the four was holding his gun...

Finding
Harmon Leete

Where were you when the birth of leaves
breathed life into the night?
Where, when the solstice moon drew silver music
through the mist?
Where were you when beneath black canopies
the pulse of captive stars ringed secret beds?

Now at the end of summer you have come
and I have bent time backwards to embrace you,
contending in defense of hubris
that you were brought beside my life

unfairly and too late
and that your gathering but repays a debt,
completes a whole
as fragile as the rainbow
I now touch.

Before It's Light
Lyn Lifshin

I lie here, thinking
how much more
seems over even
now, with crocus
petals in the snow.
Once in New York
I sat and felt sun
burn my pale thighs
another March as
snow pulled away.
Then, even burning
with loss, I thought
of what would
unwind, slam west,
whose arms would soon hold me.

128

Past-Prime Pageant
Ellaraine Lockie

Her name is Naomi LaMere. Artist femme fatale with long, straight hair and black leather fringed jacket. Ten years away from hormonal bruises. Sexy in a sixties' way to the men on our ski trip. My husband is no exception. His eyes rivet to fringe.

"Forty max and lookin' good," according to a New Yorker. Of the male variety, of course.

I'm back in junior high when Kimmy Fisher gets the highest bid on her picnic basket. I return to the "fuck" that falls from Naomi's red lips. And to men hopeful that the real thing might follow.

It's my throne she's sitting on. The fur ski hat her crown. When did I transfer it? There's supposed to be a ceremony. Never mind; the contest is over. The vote was silent, unanimous. Miss Ski Trip 2005.

My reign ends. Repealed by my own body: hair too brittle for length, double chin shadows, give-away wrinkles. I'm back in memories of title years with more than my share of high bids. Pound for pound, a 4-H heifer at auction. Always winning the blue ribbon. Sold to the highest bidder once, for trophy reasons. A disastrous transaction.

I return to my second husband's whisper. He likes my curly hair. Take it from here, Naomi. Kimmy, too, wherever you are.

Explaining the Heart
Paul Martin

These frozen months no word
rose to the blank page
I faced each morning.
Absent-minded, I drew
flat lines and three dimensional boxes.
Then came that day in early April
when I emerged
coatless into the warm air
to sit on the swing under the mulberry tree.
After a while I closed my notebook
and stopped trying.
I began watching for you
to come around the pond.
That's when I noticed the gold
high in the dying willow,
the bright notes in the redbird
bouncing from one bare
limb to another.
The sweetness of damp earth
rose and fell in my chest
and there, on the arm of the swing,
was an old hand
impressing a heart in the soft wood
with a pen.
With each retracing raising it
and then, indifferent to my embarrassment,
inscribing your initials
and mine inside it.

Auditing the Heart
Frank Matagrano

One mother who owned
   the sea, one father who walked

on water, and in a row boat,
   one brother who believed

marriage meant becoming
   the roof over a woman's head.

A room for the night with a view
   of the water, the moon a quarter

less than it should have been,
   the shape of my wife drawn

into the empty bed one memory
   at a time. There were too many

stars to count, a registry
   of old gifts and receipts strewn

across the sky, a mess
   of things that died getting here.

132

Shannon Stood
Candice Mayes

At Tiff's 24th birthday party, Shannon stood in front of me, holding a beer, looking like a lost poodle, scrunched into her body. This new, skinny body was not as fit for scrunching as the chubby body had been. (She does this, she tucks into herself, like hiding.) She was distant and close and happy to see me and I think sad I was not as happy to see her. So I let her in, gave her an opportunity: an invitation to the hospital when this baby finally leaves my body to enter the world. (And that day that baby, that belly was so heavy as my good ole high school friends pranced about in their tank tops). Though I already knew my body would be too tired to want her there, I already knew that I would want no one, nothing at the hospital but Steve, my children, and sleep.

So why invite Shannon, who is not even a friend anymore, who I am no longer obligated to accommodate? I believe it is for the past, for what we were: drunk and loud, obnoxiously so, and never best friends though we kept our secrets. There was always a distance between us no matter how close, which made it easy to truly love and then walk away. (In my thinking, it was she who walked away as she has always walked away; she does this; she abandons.) But that day, at Tiffany's birthday party, Shannon stood, and she looked lovely but for the color of her hair. It did not match her skin, too light, like fried orange tomatoes. I have not loved many as I loved her.

133

White Roses
John McBride

You talk and it starts to rain, a fine mist.
I can't confuse your words with cloudbursts.
They spread evenly, like bright beads
upon my weeping willow.

Still, the sun's the sun, the moon,
the moon- those great bells of time –
they won't cease to toll –
I respect your decision.

These small drops fill basins, you observe.

Basins that become fountains
and make a lovely show,
and then are turned off for winter,
grey ice gripping the naiads.

You say you have heard about that time,
the time of white roses,
that comes like a ghost into the room,
that comes to watch one die, well,

it won't be me or you – let's
not run or hide,
and love may, just may
bloom fresh for us
a second time.

Love Remains
Kathy McElligott

A young mother yearns for her husband's embrace
Exhausted, she falls asleep in his arms
And dreams of his warm kiss
An infant cries plaintively, edging her consciousness
Honey, the baby's awake, he says nudging her
She slips into sleep while her child suckles

Lock the door she laughs as they fall into bed
Recalling the taste of passion
Tearing off clothes, they feast on urgent kisses
Outside the bedroom door a child's voice rises:
Mommy, are you in there?
Where are you, Mommy?

She paces the floor at 2:00 AM
Their son's curfew is 12:30
Come to bed he calls from upstairs
But she continues, thinking the worst
How can he sleep, she wonders,
Her third cup of coffee cold in her hand

In a house now quiet
She stares at the grandchildren's photos
Amazed at her good fortune
He massages her shoulders, kisses her neck
Stirring up memories of passion –
Love remains

136

Girl Lover
Jeanne Miller

A boy face pops through the doorway
banishing old questions of loving males.
Intent on loving me till infinity.
Nothing can be higher, he insists.
More than cartoons, even cantaloupe,
he pinky swears. I'm yours.
Seven-year-old devotee to the shrine of me
hugging arms, enfolded   we
read in a space created for two
swirl in a swoon still brand new to this girl lover
who once wondered if she could love a son
enough.

138

How To Get Away with Murder
Elaine Ruth Mitchell

My obsession with murder began on *Rosh Hashanah*, the Jewish New Year, when I looked across the crowded room of our synagogue and saw him. He was tall, dark, and so handsome as he swayed in prayer that I wanted to rush across the aisle dividing the women from the men, climb under his *tallis*, and sway with him.

Love at first sight. A bolt out of the blue.

Or a bolt out of the unconscious? He looked the way my father must have looked in his mid-forties, just before he left my mother. He resembled my grandfather (the womanizer of Warsaw) as he appeared in the old brown and white photos.

I turned to my friend, Brenda, who knew everybody and thought she knew everything.

"Two seats from the aisle in the fourth row," I whispered. "The one with the strong and sensitive face."

"Forget it," she whispered back. "He's trouble. Jake Golden. Unhappily married but he'll never leave his wife."

"Why not?" Standing there, yearning before the open ark, I couldn't believe how much I wanted that man.

"Guilt. She put him through medical school, and then raised their five children while he became a star surgeon."

I dug my fingers into my palms to manage sudden mad anxiety. "How do you know he'll never leave her?"

"I tried," she said. Bitterly?

"You never told me."

She shrugged and tossed her head, tipping her rhinestone-studded beret to one side. "You were such a prude when you were married." She sighed.

"Sshh!" hissed Carol Greene.

If he won't leave his wife, then I'll have to kill her. The thought surprised me but didn't shock. For years, my fantasies had been not of extra-marital sex but of inter-marital murder. Still, as I touched the Torah and kissed my fingers, I was a little unnerved by such an immediate leap to the removal of a stranger's hard-working wife.

Of course, I didn't mean it. After the ark was closed, I started thinking of how I could meet Jake. (Everyone else was probably counting the ways to live an ethical Jewish life in the coming year.) I stared at Jake again, tried to see if I could make him look at me, but he just kept swaying.

Lunch at the Library!

I was working part time at a library which asked guests, ranging from rap singers to social activists, to speak and take part in a monthly community lunch. When I called Jake at his office with an invitation, he said, in a voice deep and thrilling, "I'd love to come."

I'd love to help you come.

⟡

I tried on every piece of clothing I owned for that lunch, finally choosing a respectable-yet-sexy black knit dress. "What are you doing," asked my 15-year-old daughter, Abbie, when she wandered into my room for a pair of socks that morning. "Why is your entire wardrobe on the bed?"

Before I left the house, I dabbed Chanel No. 5 behind my ears and between my breasts. Rushed to the library staff room. No one there – they were all in the Round Room, preparing for the lunch. I, of course, had volunteered to greet the guest.

"Why are you staring at me?" he asked.

"I think you're gorgeous," I said. It was the bravest act of my life, telling him that. He grinned. "Thank you. From someone as beautiful as you – that's a real compliment."

The first time we made love was so different and better than anything I'd experienced that I thought I could die then and there from happiness.

And then I thought – *Better his wife should die.* Painlessly, of course. To get my mind off sex and death, I rolled off of Jake and asked him about his childhood.

"I don't remember it," he said.

I asked him about his marriage.

"We can't talk to each other," he said.

He and I could talk to each other. We talked all the time. We talked when we had dinner together (at remote and unknown restaurants), we talked on the phone as often as we could, and we talked before lovemaking, after lovemaking, and during journeys to unusual erotic venues (metaphorical – we were always on his office couch).

"This is the best sex I've ever had," he told me one night. "And what's more," he said when he could talk again, "I like you so much."

Cyanide? An overdose of sleeping pills? I couldn't imagine killing her with a gun or a knife.

I couldn't imagine killing her at all, although I imagined it all the time. Aside from a lifetime of relentless niceness, I didn't have the skills. But I was a reader, a good researcher. I went to at least 10 libraries in the city, and read or flipped through at least 40 books.

I read about detection, forensics, poisons, and true crime. Skimmed mystery novels for specific details about poisoning someone. I learned that a lot of people get away with murder, but I didn't get any real knowledge of how to commit a murder, or of what happens afterwards.

Not that I was going to do it.

⟡

When Abbie came across the books in my room – she had been searching for my black cashmere sweater – I told her that I wanted to write a murder mystery. "My therapist thinks it's a good idea," I improvised. "Another way to integrate my shadow side."

"Whatever," said Abbie.

"A novel about a woman who kills her husband," I said. Maybe I actually would write a book.

"You could ask the police for help," said Abbie. "You might meet a cute cop."

With one phone call, by announcing that I was a writer, I was able to make an appointment to visit police headquarters and interview a staff-sergeant, no less.

"Why did you choose Homicide?" I started the interview. Staff-Sergeant Rogers was definitely cute in a clean-cut, boyishly blond way. He hadn't asked for my credentials.

"If you want to be a detective, it's the pinnacle." He hadn't even asked for ID.

"What happens when you first learn of a murder?" I leaned towards him.

"We go to the scene. We record everything, take photos, question everybody there."

"Do you question everyone connected with the victim?"

"Everyone," he said huskily as his denim blue eyes gazed into mine. "Even people with only slight connections. You never know when someone will say something important, or let something slip."

141

I hadn't told anyone but Brenda about my affair with Jake.

Of course, I didn't have to worry since Jake's fleshy wife wouldn't actually be reduced to a chalk outline on their living room carpet.

So how was I to get my man? If Homicide was the pinnacle for a detective, then Jake was the pinnacle for me. Not only did I adore him, he was a great catch, a better catch than my ex-husband who would choke on the news that I was remarrying someone like Jake.

What would I do with my life if I didn't get Jake? How could being a part-time librarian, shopper, mother, and friend be enough? Beneath my performative autonomy, I secretly believed that without a husband I'd just be putting in time until I died.

"How come you're in such a good mood?" asked Abbie when I got back to the house.

"I had an interesting day doing research for my book." I told her about my trip to Homicide.

"I'm glad you're doing something like this. You've been really weird lately."

The next time I was with Jake, he introduced a new motif into our lovemaking. He tied me up with surgical gauze and led me through a version of playing doctor that produced how many orgasms? Twenty or thirty, maybe. *Nothing matters but this*, I remember thinking.

142

I was still flying the next day and I found myself with so much positive energy needing to do something that I sat down at the computer and began to write. The words came easily in the first person, from the point of view of the murderer. She was Chloe Lundy, a frustrated North Toronto housewife, and I wanted people to understand why she needed to murder her husband.

I wrote for six hours without stopping.

"How come there's no supper, Mom?"

"I've been working," I said proudly.

The following day I spent four and a half hours on my book.

When I next met my staff-sergeant, he took me out for breakfast at Fran's, half a block away from police headquarters.

"Do you have shifts?" I asked him.

"Days it's eight to four, and afternoons four to twelve. But we could work right through a tough case."

"Don't you get exhausted?" He looked fresh and healthy.

"I've gone for 30 hours with no sleep. The initial thrust is so important that the lead team is divorced from everything else."

"Interesting language."

"Thrust?"

"Divorced," I answered demurely.

"You're not wearing a wedding ring," he said.

"I've been separated for a year."

He leveled his gaze at mine. "I admire you for writing a book at this point in your life."

"Thanks." It wasn't hard to look modest and embarrassed. "So, tell me, why don't you have a woman officer on the Squad?"

"If this is a test, I can pass with flying colors. I have a mother whose bookcases could supply a women's studies department at any university. I put my ex-wife through law school."

He was truly nice and he didn't talk like a cop.

"So, uh, do you usually catch your man?" I asked, deliberately avoiding gender neutral.

"Usually. He's only done it once and we've seen it all."

"What kind of mistakes does he make?"

"You name it. Leaving physical clues. Talking too much. Maybe someone else talks too much. Or we find something because we're patient and thorough. One of the reasons we work so hard at the beginning is that we try to get to everyone connected to the victim and record their statements before they can make up an alibi or work up a lie."

That night I got so involved in my book that I didn't get to sleep until 2:00. Writing gave me a high. The words seemed to come through me rather than from me, and I loved the way ideas and memories rushed from the corners of my mind to connect in surprising sentences.

I loved Chloe, my murderess, a brave woman trying to find herself through volunteer work and murder.

It didn't take long before I had to write every day, or I felt edgy, guilty almost. And there was pleasure in not knowing exactly what was going to happen, or what Chloe would do. I was finding out what I was thinking by writing. It was a great adventure, a more elegant game even than therapy.

Making love was another great adventure. And fun. What a good time I was having, day and night. I hadn't had such a time in 20 years.

"Enjoy," said Brenda during the Passover service. "But don't even think about marrying him. He's a man to go to bed with, not to make your bed with."

"Shhh!" hissed Carol Greene, who should have known better than to sit behind us.

To background chanting, I mused on my one big problem, aside from unreliable support payments. I hadn't been able to figure out how Chloe could kill her husband.

I was stuck. Writer's block. And I wasn't even a real writer.

Meanwhile, Jake was starting to repeat himself in bed. There are only so many positions, and he didn't seem to want to act out any more fantasies.

"The thing is, I love you," he told me. "That sort of thing doesn't seem appropriate when you really love someone."

After a night with Jake that gave me only three orgasms, and a day at my keyboard in which nothing came out, I knew I needed help.

"I'm glad you called me," Staff-Sergeant Rogers said. "I think about you a lot."

"I have a problem with the book."

"Oh, sure," his voice flattened. "Shoot."

I reached over and squeezed his arm. "I need a poison that leaves no trace and doesn't kick in for hours after ingesting."

"Digitalis." His rushed intonation revealed an ardent desire to help me.

"How would an ordinary person get it?" I curbed my own eagerness by slowing my voice. "My protagonist is just a housewife."

"Go to Forensics." He wrote a number on his card and handed it to me.

"Thanks. I was wondering – have you ever felt any sympathy for a murderer?"

"Yes. But as an officer, if I don't act as the victim's advocate, then who will?"

"I see that you have to believe that, but I think that some murders are justified. Don't take that the wrong way."

He didn't. He asked me out to dinner on Saturday night. I said I'd think about it.

With Jake the next evening it was just like the early days. Almost unbearable pleasure and the sense of being intensely connected to him, the feeling of being more alive than I ever had been before.

I asked him to leave his wife.

"I can't live without you, but I can't leave her." I could hear the high whine of his desperation.

—◆—

The Assistant Director at Forensics had been helpful. I knew how to kill her.

In the last, mad, sleepwalking stage of my obsession, while Jake was napping on the office couch after making love, I got up to poison the container of guacamole that he had purchased especially for his wife, having lifted some of my uncle's heart pills and processed them into powdered digitalis in the Cuisinart that morning.

But I didn't do it. I couldn't be that crazy. I left Jake sleeping and went home to write. I never saw him again. Cold turkey.

◆

I had to change synagogues. Was lucky to find a breakaway *minion* where the men and women sat together and gender was clearly a construct anyway, and where grey ponytails hung above tie-dyed *tallisim*, the rabbi was pre-op, the congregation still working and hoping for peace in Israel, and divorced women writers were pillars instead of pariahs.

I finished my book and got it published by a women's press operating out of Vancouver. I started a second novel.

And I found the perfect lover in Staff-Sergeant Rogers. His being a Younger Man, his not being Jewish Husband Material, freed me from my conditioned response to men. We took turns playing a homicide officer who sleeps with the chief suspect. Took turns owning the keys to the handcuffs. He was always at the ready, always up for anything, always totally into me. But, best of all for a writer, shift work kept him from being underfoot.

146

Chicago Fog
Leana Page

Gayle stumbled from the bedroom to the front door wondering who could possibly be ringing her doorbell so early in the morning. Sleepless hours followed by a sleeping pill had given her a drug-induced headache. Somewhat off balance, she held onto the walls and negotiated the narrow hallway. It was just another day in the journey towards recovery she'd been told would take time. With each painful step she took, she doubted the words of the rape crisis therapist. How could such a professional have been so dismissive of the anguish she was still experiencing?

A look through the peephole revealed Lonnie standing on the porch carrying the biggest toolbox she'd ever seen. It put the one she had been building to shame. Dressed in jeans and an old shirt, he stood there bouncing from one foot to the other. Gayle smiled as she recognized that nervous energy he always had trouble hiding. Over the years she'd seen him off and on, but generally from a distance as he'd thickened and grown into a very handsome, strong-limbed man.

"You're early," she said almost apologetically as she opened the door and attempted to smooth down her hair. She pulled the belt on her robe taut while she backed into the hallway and turned to make her way towards the kitchen. "It's this way," she said as she flipped on light switches and they moved towards the rear of the house. She led him to the kitchen sink where that endlessly dripping faucet had gotten on her last nerve. She felt embarrassed for the cluttered room, which was in the middle of her current rehabbing phase.

She got caught up in the shy little grin he flashed her as he put his toolbox down on the floor. It caused her to flush as a warm feeling passed over her.

"Well, what seems to be the problem?" he asked, trying to put her at ease. He'd agreed to help out when his sister had called him and explained how desperate Gayle was to get the sink fixed.

On a better day she would probably have attempted to fix it herself. Although she had become an avid do-it-yourself fix-it machine,

147

she still shied away from electrical and plumbing problems, allowing herself to stay well within her comfort zone with cosmetic cleanup jobs. Only been in the last six months had she attempted to work with power tools. And she'd found that she was a natural.

Gayle watched Lonnie as he stole glances around the room. She tucked a lock of hair behind her ear in an effort to hide a strand of gray. She mentally examined herself and decided that she was still attractive although it was 20 years since she'd been in high school. She had in fact aged well; very well, right down to the flat stomach that she'd had when she played tennis in the neighborhood park two decades earlier.

"Listen, Gayle, I need to run out to my truck and pick up another tool box. It'll just take me a minute," he said

"I'll pull on some clothes while you're gone," she said. "I need some coffee to get rid of this headache."

"Not to worry. I'll get this drip out of here in no time," he said as he strode across the floor and headed for the front door.

"Wait, could I ask you to do me a big favor?"

"What's that?"

"Show me how to install this new faucet. Or I'll pay you if you go ahead and do it. I bought it months ago and meant to put it in myself. I just never got around to it," her voice trailed off as she remembered another time in her life when moving ahead was important to her. "I mean, if you have time today."

"Sure," he said. "I still need my other tool box – be back in a second. You stay put. I'll let myself out."

"I have to put some coffee on," she mumbled, watching his retreating back and feeling a twinge as she remembered their teenage years and she'd been coerced into tutoring him to keep him from failing algebra. She could never be sure, but she always thought that he was smarter than a lot of people gave him credit for, and just lazy when it came to schoolwork.

They'd shared a first kiss then: an open mouth kiss with tongue that was new and exciting for her. She was convinced that it was the best secret she'd ever share with anyone until the neighborhood kids started to tease her. He'd told his best friend who betrayed both of them. Gayle had been embarrassed and afraid of being labeled a bad girl. But more than that, it was a treasured moment she could no longer solely claim. There had not been a second kiss; just bashful and sometimes shameful glances across crowded rooms. Still, that kiss remained the standard by which she measured all others.

After setting the coffee to brew, she went to the bedroom to slip on some clothes. Gayle caught sight of the six-month-old scar on her arm; still repulsed by it, she pulled on a sweatshirt to cover it up. When will this be just a memory, she wondered as she yanked on the tattered jeans. She had taken to dressing quickly without looking in the mirror. Today she'd made the mistake of seeing herself with the disturbing scar.

She'd made another change and that was to quit her job. It was hard to let go of the practical side of what she'd been taught. Excelling in the world had been her focus for most of her life. Initially she had fought to hold onto that life. She'd been determined not to let the violence take away what she'd worked so hard to build.

The rape had left Gayle feeling so vulnerable that staying close to home was her way of coping. She'd practically removed herself from the social scene and turned her thoughts and efforts inward – working on developing herself further, searching not so much for enlightenment as finding her purpose in life. She'd finally opted out of the banking business in search of a more authentic self. Each day she was learning to truly simplify her life by de-cluttering the space she lived in as well as her entourage of friends and acquaintances. She forced herself to resume as much of her life as she felt safe to do. For a while she didn't share the experience beyond the family out of fear of the gossip that generally goes along with people who have suffered a misfortune. She looked at the world and the people in it with new eyes. After a time she was finally able to see clearly who mattered in her life and know who would be there to comfort her when she cried until all her fluids dried up and she found herself exhausted.

On the "keep list" was her friend, Monica, and it was Monica's brother, Lonnie, who was helping out because she had sent him. He could be trusted because Monica could be trusted.

When Lonnie returned he said, "All right, where's the new faucet?"

She looked directly into those eyes of his that had always captivated her and felt a little flushed as her body reacted to the kindness of them. Perhaps darker than she remembered, his green eyes fit so perfectly in the face that now was strong and masculine with a squarish chin lightly stubbled. All the hairs were even and she was certain that he'd trimmed them with scissors.

Lonnie took the new faucet and started reading the instructions.

"That fog is thick out there," she said as she stumbled to the kitchen window. "Springtime can do that."

"Yeah, it was a little hard to see through it on the trip over," said Lonnie. "I drove along Lake Shore Drive and could barely see the shores of Lake Michigan. And you know how close the lake is to the Drive."

"You could have come another day. I mean, it wasn't an emergency or anything," Gayle said.

"Well, Monica said it was important to get it fixed for you."

He continued to talk as he knelt in front of the cabinet containing the sink. At first it was general stuff about the warmer weather, old classmates, and everyday things. He realized that he was getting only one-word answers from her so he inhaled and made motions with his hands to indicate confusion over the instructions. He furrowed his brow, clicked his teeth, and then resumed the conversation with more determination. He had decided to push on to the more substantive thing that he'd wondered about. "So, Gayle," he said, "what are you doing these days?"

"Considering my options," she said just above a whisper with confusion and despair permeating her voice.

"Yeah, life can be a little hard sometimes," he dared to tread. With the faucet installed, he stood and turned the water faucets on one at a time. "But at least you'll have water."

"You're done already. That was fast. You know, I've found out that I'm good with my hands, too," she said, slightly embarrassed. Although she'd had a successful career in corporate banking, she had sometimes felt overwhelmed in trying to conform to the old mores and values she'd once thought important. "I traveled another road," she said, "only to find that I wanted to do something else all the time," feeling as if somehow that was not enough for an old friend. She'd reverted to a self-imposed shyness of late which reminded her of how she had been when growing up. The world seemed too big for her then and she became an introvert concentrating on her books. It still made her feel small, but at least she was able to control her environment more – with the exception of the life-changing event that had occurred six months earlier.

"Yeah, I heard you had become a banker. Is that right?" He'd made it his business to know about her and everything she did over the years, with the exception of the single year he'd been married. It was during that time that he'd given up hope of ever being the one man in her life.

"I was in banking when I first left school," she volunteered. With a second thought, she added, "Well, that was what I used to do. I'm taking time off work to figure out what I really want to do."

"How's that?" he asked. "You didn't like the world of big finance."

"It was fine for a while. I was good at it. Numbers always came easy for me. But now I just need something different."

"Oh yeah, why is that?" Lonnie looked down into Gayle's face.

Gayle looked away from him so that he could not see the glassy effect the sleeping pills had left in her eyes. She knew that she'd lost the clarity that normally showed through her eyes. She felt him as he moved towards her and gently reached for her hands. She pulled back before she realized she'd reacted like a scared child. She was afraid. There was no denying that.

"You're still running from me after all these years," he whispered. He placed his left hand under her chin and held her face up towards his. "What can I do to make it better for you?"

"You're helping me right now," she said. "Just being a good friend means so much to me. Would you like to stay awhile? We could talk," she ventured to say. "I could make us some breakfast. Do you like pancakes? I should probably stop eating them. Lately they've been the thing that comforts me. Well, it at least gets me out of bed some mornings, knowing that I can have them. Or maybe you'd prefer waffles?"

She looked into his eyes and without knowing why she took her hands and placed them on his cheeks. She looked into his green eyes and found tranquility in not only the color, but also the cool restful look of the big, gentle giant that stood before her. "Well, I've thought about you over the years and just thought that you were, I don't know, too much for me. I mean you were one of those bad boys in the 'hood."

151

"I don't know about bad. Maybe just searching for something."

"You were married for awhile. Monica told me," she said as an opening for more conversation. She wanted to know more about the man he'd become as she dropped her hands from his face, making room for his response.

"Didn't last – wasn't meant to last. We married for all of the wrong reasons. After Edie lost the baby, there was nothing to really hold us together. I suppose it was more than either of us could handle alone or as a couple."

Her eyes widened in sympathy. "It must have been a horrible experience for you."

"It took a while for me to wrap my mind around it and move on. Sometimes I see something and it brings me up short. Then I'm back mourning it all over again."

"They say it gets a little easier with time," said Gayle with so little conviction that it startled her. "Let's just say that sometimes life throws you unexpected curves," she said as she nodded her head and felt more grounded in those words. The phrase had become her mantra, the way she opened up her mind for new experiences. It was what allowed her to close the door on old ones that she no longer wanted to control her life.

"Pancakes?" he said as his shy little grin surfaced. "Real butter?"

"Yeah." She smiled broadly. "Real butter."

"Good trade. Faucet installation for a plate of pancakes," he reasoned with a little nod. "That's a deal I can't turn down."

"Right," she said. "Sit down and stay a while."

"I'm not going anywhere," he said. "Maybe we can just spend a little time getting reacquainted. I can't say that I've seen much of you in the past few years. There used to be a time when we'd bump into each other every now and then. But not lately." He gazed at her hesitantly for a moment, then let that smile return to light his face.

Gayle glanced away toward the kitchen window where she could see the spring fog lifting over the backyard. The season of rebirth was about to begin.

For Those Who Wait
Natalie Pepa

Renata learned how to wait when she was a child. All the brothers came first; that was the rule in the house. So she learned to wait for her turn at the table, her turn for gifts at Christmas, her permission to leave the house after the chores. She even learned to wait for that which never came. It was a good lesson – this eternal postponement of gratification – it taught her not to expect the fulfillment of promises.

With time, the waiting transformed into yearning, the first part of which was simply to turn 10 so she could walk to her friend's house by herself. Later, it was to grow up and fill out like the rest of her girlfriends, who had matured before her. Then to fall in love and then to recover. After that it was some mysterious longing she felt as acutely as the pounding of her heart. She welcomed the restlessness and sadness for they became a substitute for what she did not have. It made her feel superior, this profound melancholy of poets.

When she married, all her wishes seemed fulfilled and the waiting was simply for the children to be born, for dinner to cook, for the house to be built. It was all so mundane, she no longer called it yearning. There was no excuse for melancholy. For the next 20 years she behaved like a proper suburban wife – chauffeuring the children, entertaining her husband's business associates, shopping with her friends.

Inside, the sadness continued to churn. She would awaken in the middle of the night, move away from David, and cry softly, not understanding her own tears. When David asked for a divorce, Renata was relieved – there was reason now to feel sad. She was left with the large house and generous alimony. She could have sold the house and moved anywhere, but chose to remain in San Francisco close to two of her children. One daughter, unmarried, had moved to the East Coast and Renata visited her frequently.

She was there now, in the middle of summer, spending the day in Kensington, a quaint town with narrow streets lined with antique shops. Renata stopped at a little café for lunch and crossed the outdoor patio, keenly aware of a man sitting by himself at a table in the corner. Quickly she took him in, felt the chemistry, so sudden and indiscriminating. She stopped to look at the menu on the wall, then fumbled through her purse.

"Here, take mine," the man said, offering his glasses.

She looked at him and smiled, then retrieved her glasses and waved them in the air.

"Thanks, I've got them."

He had a rough face, like one exposed and at ease with the elements and a gentleness perhaps because of the white beard, the rimless glasses. When he turned his head, she saw his white hair pulled back in a pony tail. So much of him reminded her of David – the good of David. Though how could she know whether his blue eyes could also turn to stone. But this afternoon, the eyes were soft and deeply questioning.

It had been some time since she'd seen that look in any man. Perhaps, she had to acknowledge, she had simply shut her eyes to it. After David left, she had gone through several failed love affairs that took her ever deeper into the old sadness. As if David's departure had left an open wound that grew larger with each disappointment. Even the slightest rejection – a broken date by a new man, another's failure to call after a concert, a friend's promise of a blind date that never materialized – all these seemingly innocuous incidents were magnified in her mind, enlarged the wound, made it fester like gangrene. Finally after the last hurtful breakup, more than two years before, she had decided to stop looking.

Renata took a table next to the man and ordered a salad and an iced tea. Even before the waitress came, he engaged her in conversation. It happened so innocently she could hardly be upset with what could be construed as a pass.

"You must be a dancer," he said, "you have legs like Betty Grable."

"Sure, from the old movies," she said. "And I do like dancing."

He, Hank something (later she could not recall his last name), told her he lived in Kensington, that he had three grown children and four grandchildren. They spoke through the whole meal about life in general, the current political problems, the attractions in the area. His voice was soft, and he knew so much about everything, like David, who would read at least five books a week. Hank's attentiveness was irresistible.

"I love antiques," she told him.

"Great, I'm an antique." They both laughed.

If you give me a half a chance, Renata thought, *I could grow to love you.*

"The place is full of them. If you start over there," he pointed to the right, "two blocks full of shops."

She was so sure he would ask for her phone number or to meet him later, that when he got up from his meal and went inside to pay, she expected him to return with a piece of paper. Instead, he returned with two singles which he placed under his cup, then turned to Renata again with that look of extreme interest.

"If you were living here," he said, "I'd build a wooden dance floor just for you."

She wanted to tell him that she had no attachment to her home in San Francisco, that one coast was as good as another, that she was simply waiting for the right reason to move. But she only smiled, acknowledging the indirect complement, and told him she had enjoyed their conversation. He expressed the same, shook her hand, and then was gone.

Renata sat for a long time stunned by what felt like a betrayal, trying to understand the rejection. But was it rejection? Was he a shy man who did not know how to take the next step? Perhaps he was turned off by the fact that she was not local. What if he had read her signals wrong and believed she was not interested? Had she not done that so many times before – put up a protective wall that turned men away? She became angry at herself for staying in her passive role. What would have been wrong in asking him for *his* number?

She returned the next day at noon, sat in the same spot, ordered the same meal. If he lived in the neighborhood, she might meet him again. A level voice inside reasoned that if she could not find him, destiny did not mean for it to be. But – God helps those who help themselves, another voice said. Though she did not believe in God *per se*, she did believe in a concept of a greater power in charge of human lives. If I put myself in the proper place, it's a clue that I am taking positive steps and that "it" ought to help me, she reasoned. She wanted to ask the waitress if she knew him, but it was a different girl and she had no idea who the man was.

"Ask the owner of the card shop on the corner," the girl said. "She knows everyone."

But the shop owner did not know him either.

Renata remained there for some time and ended up buying a vintage card, taking a long time to decide on one. She wanted something with meaning, but not too much meaning. There was one of two lovers sitting on a park bench in the glow of moonlight, another of a flapper dancing, many with animals and children. She settled on one of a woman in profile, a long dress from the late nineteenth century, gazing over a harbor where in the distance two galleons were either coming at or away from each other. The woman on shore was obviously waiting.

I RETURNED TO KENSINGTON TO PICK UP AN ANTIQUE I'D SEEN YESTERDAY.

She did not want him to believe, though it was true, that she had returned only to find him. She wanted to make the note brief, neither too revealing nor too cold.

I ENJOYED OUR CONVERSATION YESTERDAY AND FELT SAD WE DID NOT EXCHANGE NUMBERS. HERE IS MY VERSION OF THE LETTER IN A BOTTLE CAST INTO THE SEA. IF IT REACHES YOU, HERE IS MY NUMBER.

She drew a picture of him on the envelope. A caricature of a gentle man with glasses, a beard, and a pony tail. She wrote "Hank" in large letters and sealed the envelope.

"If you see this man, please give it to him," she told the waitress as she handed it to her with a generous tip. "Please don't throw it away," she added, before walking away.

She felt strange about pleading with this young woman, a stranger, who suddenly held her future in her hands. Would the girl simply laugh and throw the note away? Or did the girl, like Renata herself, also believe in waiting. Neither of them understood yet that only the waiting endures.

Years later when the incident was only a sad and poignant memory for Renata, and her yearning for love had dwindled, the card remained – picture and name easily visible – pinned to the wall behind the cashier. Eventually, it would turn yellow with age, growing old like the picture inside, like the text itself, adrift on the vast whiteness of the wall, waiting for someone to find it.

Saving Grace
Nancy Rafal

*P*rivate services will be held, read the newspaper obituary. The text had been ready for a month. She had gone into decline, then lingered, finally existing purely on the energies of her caregivers and her own inner grace.

Her children, who hadn't seen that grace when she was younger, were surprised at the ways it was shown. Who'd have thought that an 84-year-old woman, deaf, drugged on morphine, pained to the bone, would be so in tune that she took the towel given to her to clench away the pain and placed it between her legs so as not to piss the bed sheets. How amazing was that? This woman, who'd not eaten a bird-size morsel in days, elegantly picked up the terry cloth, slid it down her body and did not wet the bed in her urgency.

Nora recalled when she had been a teenager and first realized her mother was distant and unwilling to express affection. Nora agonized over this knowledge and the lack of physical contact with the woman who birthed her. She envied other girls whose mothers hugged them, combed their hair, tussled with them. As soon as the first man approached, Nora escaped with him only to find herself in another kind of cold existence. He made it easy for her to not see the family though they were just two hours away on the interstate. Over time a pattern of two annual visits to the parents and one in return developed and was sustained.

Nora had tried writing letters and went from lengthy handwritten epistles to computer-spawned pages while her mother went from little notes to clipped recipes to nothing. Nora tried to keep on writing, but found it difficult when she got no replies. What a shock to find all those letters squirreled away when it came time to clean out the house.

Telephone calls were scarce and painful. When Nora called, her mother had nothing to say. When her mother called, she had nothing to tell Nora. Nora could chat more with some anonymous telemarketer than she could with her own flesh and blood. How odd to find out that the mother had been active for over a decade in a public speaking group, or so the tucked away award certificates indicated.

Nora had retired from teaching. The state had made an offer she couldn't refuse. Within a couple of years, the man who'd made it easy to keep distance died, and Nora drove the interstate to the family homestead. No hugs, no tears, no talk. Nora began awkwardly to ask questions but got no answers. Mother wouldn't even reveal their wedding date. It was as if she'd locked her mouth and thrown away the key. When the step-dad died, Nora thought she'd have another chance with her mother. But this woman who'd kept her life a secret, who'd held her children at arm's length, who was conveniently deaf for many years – or not – played her last card: Lung cancer, already well advanced in her bones.

Hospice was called and soon a hospital bed, drugs, and support arrived. Nora learned from her sister that mother had given much of the family history to the hospice social worker. The marriage date had never been revealed because sister was conceived out of wedlock. How crappy was that, not to let your children throw a big anniversary party for you just because of sex before marriage? But also revealed was the fact that Mother herself was the product of a one-night stand when her own mother was 29. The man took off for the West Coast when he was told he was going to be a father. They found a letter in the grandmother's unmistakable hand stating he'd never married. Nora and her sister became caregivers. In four months they touched and handled this woman they knew as their mother more than they had before in their entire lives. They bathed her, clothed her, cut and combed her hair, fed her, caressed her, held her. They watched her wince when the pain wrenched her pelvis. She never cried out, she endured, she radiated grace. They wanted her to live, to recover, to be the mother they had never known. And they wanted her to die, to be out of her pain, out of her suffering.

158

The sisters became closer. They hugged when one sister had to fly back to her job a mosaic of states away. They hugged and wept when she returned to relieve Nora for a spell. They felt imbued with the mother's grace, and with it, new emotions welled up in themselves. Each daughter washed the woman with her tears, tears she'd kept in the cellar of her heart all these years. Each daughter watched the mother's serene eyes imploring feelings beyond the conventions of words. And the sisters finally shared secrets which explained why neither mourned the step-dad's death.

They did what was required and dosed the mother with drugs to ease pain and helped her use the commode, then the adult diapers, and finally, that towel. They gave eye droppers of water and Gatorade. They observed her daintily dabbing the escaped drops from her chin with the bed sheet. They endured her suffering as she endured it, with grace, in silence. When the sister had to leave again, Nora was left to attend this woman who'd been so private for eight decades and was now so totally exposed, and she loved her mother more than words could say.

The Briefcase Man (excerpt)
Mike Robinson

P REFACE: Ever wonder how many times the phrase 'Life After Death' has been uttered on Earth, or how many headaches the simple thought has ignited, leaving a wake of confusion and frustrated musings across our minds? It is one of the profound mysteries, sure, but its other half sits neglected and ignored, because no one scratches their contemplative melon on Life Before Birth.

Many have the impression that we were nothing before being born, that we were a gleam in our father's eye, the shadow of air. But those that think this way are, in fact, mistaken – for the road stretches far and long behind us, as much as it does ahead of us. Human life is simply a tourist stop, an event that happens and passes.

The following text chronicles the experience of a lone consciousness before it entered the skull of a human being. The original language was, of course, Thought, the intangible stream of mind that is often guised under assigned words. It has since been translated into millions of languages across the cosmos.

I realize it would help if I describe myself, but I can't, at least not in any physical sense you're used to. Therefore, I'm giving you, the Reader, complete artistic license in how your mind sees me. The words of this book...they wear my thoughts, my perceptions, and my experiences, so perhaps they will help in cobbling together some image for you to identify with.

In the meantime, here's something I whipped up: ☺
Use it if you want.

I was born like every other consciousness, as a cell of the Whole caught in a perpetual early-morning rush hour through the Universe. In this plane there is no light, no dark, only a sense of "is" and "be." We were rounded up like cattle and herded through the farm, nurtured by the indifferent hand of this mother called Chaos.

159

In my existence in the head of a human being, I have come to realize that mankind is one of the most diligent species in its quest for an ultimate purpose. Yet you all stare into the mouth of the unknown beast, intimidated by its massive teeth that drip enigma, and through it all you never stand back to see that said "beast" is nothing more than a small critter, as helpless as its children but scary only because of its oversized maw and fangs.

This quest for the ultimate purpose has inevitably brought you guys science. Now I'm not gonna knock science; it's great and very much suited to the way the human brain is arranged and ordered, but it's elementary. It's a pill to help you digest this huge spoonful of 'world' that's been shoved into your mouths. No matter how far science takes future theories, labs and technologies, humanity will never graduate past fifth grade in the Universe. This is not your species' fault – it is no one's fault; in fact, it has more to do with the limitations of your home dimension. In your years as a collective mind, you've stumbled upon quite an impressive lot of knowledge: atoms, DNA, the brewing superstring theory. But true reality will always be the woman out of the shower, wrapped in a towel and darting into the bedroom to change before anyone sees her.

So who am I, you ask? I am not a human, although I just recently worked in the head of one. I am not of any physical plane – yet my experience in the skull of an Earth man has certainly granted me a close connection with the third dimension and how it runs. It's a very sheltered corner of the Universe, to say the least.

Who am I?

I am the house of thought, emotion, and reason.

I am the stagehand behind the curtain, the voice from the stands.

I am the naked mind, disrobed of every sense; the raw batter of awareness, uncooked and lacking spices.

Consciousness.

We were all thrust into existence from the salt-shaker of nothingness. For a while there, my chums and I were free to roam the cosmos, setting out on long intergalactic journeys (our equivalent of a 'road trip,' if you will), camping out on asteroid belts and watching supernovas do their thing from afar. It was a fun time, a chaotic time – for all minds are meant to spend a millennia or two getting well-acquainted with the Universe, shaking a hand attached to an endless arm. Nourishing ourselves with knowledge and exploration, we are fattened up to ready us for the *real* journey ahead.

Although I never thought I was quite ready.

The time inevitably came for me to meet the Briefcase Man; that's what many of my chums called him at the time, since no one really knew who he was or where he came from. Some said he was the head of the Universe, the Whole, while others went so far as to say he *was* the Universe, compacted into one uniformed being that carried the fates of every conscious thing in its briefcase.

"Good eternity," he said as he approached me. I whimpered the same back to him, too nervous to sound confidently polite.

"I haven't kept you waiting long, have I? I've had so many clients, so many meetings – occasionally I lose track of time."

"N-No, I haven't been waiting long." Lose track of time? What? But you *are* time, I thought; you're everything. Or at least that's what they've all been telling me.

He inhaled stardust and exhaled galaxies. They streamed from him in visible clouds, warm breath on a frosty winter morning. The famous (or perhaps infamous?) briefcase was laid out in front of me and popped open. He spoke from behind it, as though too good to address me directly.

"You must be Diptazantarok."

"My friends call me Dip," I said over-anxiously.

"Okay..."

"Or Dipster."

"Mmm."

"Or Diphead."

"All right, I think we've covered nicknames for now."

You might've read that last line as irritated, but in fact he was not. As I said before, the Briefcase Man was everything, every leaf from the tree of existence, every color of life – and what happens when you mix all colors together? One tone: Opaque.

My confidence was steadily refilling. "How many of those brochures ya got in there, Sir?"

"There is no finite amount," the Man said, laying a few out before me. "Life is a river as endless as numbers. It rises, it falls, like bubbles growing and popping amidst a pool of acidic liquid. It occurs all over the cosmos, sometimes jailed by flesh, sometimes free-flowing and free."

I pointed to the top brochure, which pictured an icy planet set against a faded backdrop of bizarre, mammalian creatures.

"What's this place?"

"That's Depthal; it's a rather barren place." The Man flipped open the brochure and pointed to a clearer illustration of one of its hairy inhabitants. "It rarely sees sun, and many of the species see their own blood before they see any food. It's a harsh life. Usually it's the place we send minds that lack any sense of purpose or direction, so I wouldn't recommend it for you." He leaned forward, then, just to make sure, asked, "Are you at all interested?"

"Not particularly."

"All right, well, I'm gonna let you see what piques your interest. Please send any questions my way."

Leafing through the options, I stumbled across a crimson-yellow moon floating miles above a giant ringed planet (Saturn, I believe it was called). Saying nothing, I only pointed to it.

"That's Titan. It's still developing, not ready yet. Give it a few million years."

I nodded and continued through. Another red planet caught my eye, and coincidentally it was in the same solar system as Titan.

"This one?"

"Oh, the Martians – that bubble popped a long time ago." He leaned forward and plucked it from the pile. "I don't even know why that's in there anymore."

"What's this one?"

I swiped two brochures aside to get a better look at the green and blue tints that caught my attention.

The Briefcase Man sighed. I couldn't tell whether it was more out of boredom or concern. "That's Earth," he said. "It's part of the Universe's Connect-the-Dots program, although it hasn't found any other dots to connect with yet. They're still looking. I'm not sure if they'll find anything, to be honest. Some planets hide from them."

There was an intriguing gravity in his voice, a tone that beckoned as much as it prohibited. Despite the planet's intrinsic beauty, the picture on the brochure was stale, uninspired. Unlike many other planets, dimensions and realities, it hadn't shelled out too much dough for flashy advertising. I assumed it was because the brochure was a default – crafted by the Briefcase Man or his agency – to give the place some indifferent, legally-mandated chance of exposure. Every niche in the cosmos had to be presented as an option for us homeless minds.

My interest danced and played in the small picture of this Earth, a child in a sandbox, imagining possibilities.

I asked, "And they're not a bubble that has long since popped?"

"No, they're still around – for now."

"How many spots are left?"

"That's a silly question, son. Spots are constantly popping up, every second of every minute of every hour."

I nodded, my confidence dented, but not destroyed.

"Human beings are the most prominent form of life there, the most aware, but also the most intense to inhabit." He paused to cough.

"Earth is strikingly abundant with life, millions and millions of species abound. So there is much choice in the kind of consciousness you wish to become."

These human things sounded interesting. How bad could they be? I thought naively, ignorantly.

Stupidly.

Briefcase Man said, "The training program for human-mind inhabitation is quite trying and very rigorous. Of the 55 billion that enter every year, few actually make it to the third dimension and become a human consciousness." He sat back, clasping together fingers of dark space-time. The discouraging words now pushed and trampled out of the way, he followed them up with, "But you seem to have spunk, Diptazantarok, a zest for existence. That'll certainly go a long way."

He handed me another pamphlet, one much more elaborately decorated than Earth's. It was for an apartment complex, or a condominium complex, or *something*. The windows were black square pupils that glared at the world. The landscaping was extravagant, curled foliage that caressed the building like leafy mistress hands.

"What is this?"

"This," the Briefcase Man replied. "This is where you'd be undergoing your training."

"Here?" I picked up the pamphlet and began looking at it. It was only four pages of pictures, supplemented by little threads of text. They showed the courtyard, the swimming pool, one of the hallways, and several room interiors.

"Looks like a pretty decent place to spend a few centuries," I said.

The Briefcase Man ignored the comment. "Well, before we continue, I need to make sure of something."

I nodded, my gaze fixed on a picture of one of the rooms. Something about it kept my attention in militaristic line.

"I need to make sure you are, without a doubt, willing to go through with this."

"To become a human? Sure."

"Not become a human – inhabit one. You will be what makes him *him*, or her *her*. And the perquisites for such a task –"

"Yeah, yeah, I got it. Just sign me up."

My words were met with warm skepticism as they hovered between us, waiting for an acceptance from him or a retraction from me. He sat back and uprooted a thin sheet from his briefcase, doing it all very methodically, slowly, as if giving me time to stop myself.

"Look this over, then sign it," he instructed. "And read carefully, since it specifically outlines the courses you'll be taking and the situations you're liable to face."

I read the document, which appeared to be nothing but skulls and cross-bones, while he twiddled his thumbs and waited for me. On the last page, below the area for my signature, I noticed a picture of a man and woman. The Briefcase Man saw my eyes catch it and jumped on the explanation.

"Those are the landlords. I believe you've already met them in some form or another."

I nodded, recognizing the couple. The faceless woman I knew intimately – she had birthed me, had birthed all of us. The man next to her, whose features looked as structured and drab as his plaid shirt, was a distant acquaintance. I would be getting to know him.

I scribbled my signature and handed the paper back to him.

"I wish you the best of luck, Diptazantarok," the Briefcase Man said. "Honestly, I do."

"Thank you, Sir."

"I will return to see you after each stage of training, to check your progress. Remember, it is never too late to change paths, to perhaps become a housecat or something – y'know, a brain less *labyrinthine* than the one you've chosen."

"I'll be fine, Sir, thank you."

He tipped his hat, grabbed his briefcase and sank back into space, losing himself like a camouflaged soldier amidst jungle foliage. I was

left with a path in front of me: a swirling tunnel, a gateway bored into the chaos around me with the sharp and rigid drill of order. It was time to begin school.

I wish I could've said a proper good-bye to my chums, but I couldn't. Although, if they were insane like I was in choosing humanity, I might run across them someday.

Thirty-Three Days
Kimberly Rosen

J oey was one year my elder when we met. We met in the hospital. Both of us had collapsed lungs at the time. There he was, a tube in his chest, IV fluids in his arm, that antiseptic hospital scent and that plastic mattress, the bag of urine clamped to the side of his bed – and he was the prettiest thing I had ever seen. Our rooms were next to each other. I probably wasn't much of a sight, as it was my ex-boyfriend's fist that put me here, but after a week together in the hospital we were in love. The nurses cried the day he proposed. They brought me a white veil, and a few days later the hospital chaplain declared us a married couple.

We moved in together right away. I had many secrets, but Joey loved me anyway. We were something special. We teased the cops and spent time in jail. We ate liver and onions, stole cars, puffed smoke-rings and fried our brains with a pretty variety of sweets. We lived at the back door of Munjoy Hill – with Joey's son, Bud. His son's house was a smelly mess, with needles brushed under the rugs and the odor of beer and incense that never cleared despite all my efforts at cleaning. Ours was a disorganized, colorful household. Sometimes Bud played the bagpipes. Music was his only virtue, but he played up a frenzy and his parties were a riot. I sang and shrieked, pulling my skirts up and dancing on the table, and Joey clapped his hands and sniffed and laughed hysterically as I bared my panties to the world. Sometimes the neighbors joined us.

On darker nights, Joey blocked the door as I ran, just missing the drunken blows of his only son, blows that were meant for me. Bud would never hit his father. I was the easy target, bruised and bizarre and vulnerable. His father had doted over his only son until I came into the picture. But Dad was perfect. Dad was meant to love Bud and only Bud.

There were a lot of secrets. The bastard son didn't know his father was impotent and asexual. There was a lot he didn't know. I think Bud sensed it. Maybe that was why he took it out on me.

I dealt with Bud as best I could. I cooked his breakfast with rotten eggs and milk, threw a cockroach or two into his milkshakes, studied calculus out loud, and humored his stupidity with nonchalance. Mace was a good defense against his aggression. Arsenic in his drinks promoted what I hoped would be an early death.

A few months after I'd met my husband, 33 days after his 47th birthday, Joey overdosed and died. It was an accident. It had to be an accident. That was that. There was no good-bye. For a few days I stayed with Bud in his Munjoy Hill apartment, and he went on like before, only worse. He blamed me for every empty beer can that didn't make it into the garbage, blamed me for his father's death, and laughed hysterically when he brought me to tears.

I eventually slipped sedatives into his drink, bought a spicy red whore-dress for his imaginary funeral, and moved out. I sewed up the hem of my dress a few inches and bought pumps to match.

But a year later, as I sat in the back of that police cruiser on the way to the emergency room, as I repeated my story over and over to the cop who tried to care, Bud still wasn't dead. There was no funeral. I never got to spit on his grave. Yeah, if I saw Joey's son at the side of the road now, I would run him down. No doubts. But I'd gone on with life. I lived on my own now: just me and Pussy, my cat. And today I planned on ending my life.

"But why suicide?" The officer asked. That wasn't difficult: I turned 47 and 33 days today. The same age as Joey when he died. I had tried to go on as before. But I couldn't. This morning I took Pussy to the groomer. I bought a new litter box and fern plant and made plans for breakfast tomorrow with a new boyfriend. But I was crying now, on the way to the emergency room, and the officer handed me a Kleenex. His questioning was gentle, and his kind eyes willed me strength. He didn't know. No one knew. These days men were gentle with me. I had had the big vasectomy long before I met Joey – the orchiectomy, orchiotomy, castration, feminization, whatever you want to call it – and the hormones gave me the prettiest figure, delicate and limber. Yeah, the piece of boy-flesh still hung between my legs; the doctors wouldn't operate on me. But now I had the stunning effect of self-definition and independence.

Despite my tears, I chuckled at myself. Bud had turned blue that day. "What's wrong?" I had asked him. "Never tried to rape a transgender before?" He threw up in the bathroom, the bastard. That was the day I left. That was the last time I ever saw him.

So, yes, today I had groomed Pussy, cleaned the apartment, shopped for groceries – gone on with life as if it were any normal day.

But the sad plan was to dress up in that slut-red dress of mine – the one I'd bought for Bud's funeral – and wear a necklace Joey had given me. I'd put on the face, the eyelashes, those pretty pumps. Then I would take the 500 pills I'd been hoarding and finish the cycle. The officer stared off into the distance and nodded his head. I told him about the death of my love; about Bud's nasty habits and the bruises, about where we lived on Munjoy Hill (I even gave him the address), about the prettiest outfit I'd bought for Bud's funeral that never took place.

The officer laughed. He apologized for laughing. He didn't mean to be offensive. It turned out there'd recently been a police call to Munjoy Hill, to that same address I had told him. He'd been working that night and responded only to find 2 pounds of coke and a dead body: Bud's. Joey's son had shot himself in the chest. So Bud was dead, the idiot. What coincidence. We all die. Now it's my turn. We'll all fit together like a mess of dirty rags in a bucket. Ha! What imagery. The officer's eyes lingered over me. So he liked me. Maybe he didn't know. Maybe he was different.

We arrived at the emergency room.

They pushed me back into the loony-bin part of the department, and over the next four hours I talked to two social workers and a psychiatrist.

It was a big joke.

I mean I was a big joke. The shrink and I did the math. The infinite date, the one meant to close the cycle and bring me back to Joey, well, this was embarrassing, but it had come and gone: 33 days after my 47th birthday was yesterday, not today. Typical. Bud was dead and I'd outlived my suicide date. The day of reckoning had come and gone without so much as a hoot. I shrugged my shoulders and figured it was for the best.

The shrink was kind: "I guess you sort of missed the boat," he said.

"Yeah. I've always been bad at math."

"Good thing," he said. There was a pretty blue-ness in his eyes. I thought about inviting him along for breakfast tomorrow but decided against it. Yeah, men liked me these days. Maybe another time.

What now?

Looked like I was going to wear my slut-red dress to the funeral after all. And these pretty pumps. Joey wouldn't want me to miss it.

And once again, he's given me a reason to live.

168

Ucu
Lynn Veach Sadler

When my Zulu warrior jilted me,
I put by my *hlonipha* language
of respect for that mean male.

My female friends helped me
change my *ucu*,
my long necklace of white beads

wound so proudly about my neck
to tell of our engagement.
We exchanged the *ucu*'s beads for black,

its beaded tassel's blue and white
for pale yellow.
We insulted him with that *ucu*,

took it to his village.
He hid, would not come out.
We wound the insulting *ucu*

around the neck of a dog –
the first dog we met.
Then we left in withering contempt.

He knew what that new *ucu* meant –
and so did all who saw.
To keep from being branded coward,

he was forced to wear it
to my wedding to another.
He knew – and so did all the others.

170

Again: Beginning in the Middle
Shawntelle Santas

And they said it wouldn't last...on paper it's been 17 years, but the reality is hazier than the black and white of a marriage license. Technically, it's 17 years and it's a complicated math that's required to calculate how many years we've been together as opposed to how long we've been married. You can deduct the actual separations – the longest of which was eight months, and which totals two years, three months, and three weeks, give or take a day or two. It becomes more complicated when you want to adjust for all the time we've lived together alone – those times when we shared an address and not much else, when he told everyone (including, to his credit, me), we were together for financial reasons only. Then those times – should we subtract them or divide by them? – when I thought we were married, but discovered in loud and dramatic ways that he was significantly less married than I was.

Some rain fell every single day for three weeks before the wedding. Mornings dawned gray and drizzly, or sudden downpours divided sunny afternoons from damp evenings. The morning of the wedding was gloriously cloudless. We took it as A Sign. We took everything as A Sign.

The irony of getting married on the Fourth of July was not lost on me, even then, three weeks shy of my nineteenth birthday. The idea of plighting our troth, pledging our dependence on a day dedicated to celebrating Independence had its perverse pleasure. We promised to love, honor, and cherish. I promised, even after being advised by the Justice of the Peace that many couples left it out, to obey. We didn't mean it – we probably couldn't have.

They said it wouldn't last and in so many ways they were right.

These are the things I told myself when he wasn't home at 3:47 in the morning: I can't take this anymore. I won't take this anymore. I don't deserve this. Maybe he's been arrested. He should be arrested. This is completely ridiculous. The next time, I swear I'm changing the locks, forwarding his mail to Hell, dumping his crap on the front lawn for the skunks, the garbage pickers in their rusty pickups and the stray dogs to go through.

Stray dogs – how appropriate.

After the first 20 or 30 times, I no longer imagined him the victim of an especially freaky freak accident. The first few years, my inexperience and my insecurity joined forces against my common sense. I believed in his innocence and I believed in something else as well – I believed myself so unworthy of his affection that I was convinced he would be taken from me in a violent and wholly unprecedented way. Eventually I learned that when he wasn't home at midnight or one or three-something, odds were he hadn't been kidnapped by white-slave traders or eaten alive by a roving band of dingoes. (Blame it on Meryl Streep – I lived in fear of a dingo eating my baby.)

In the beginning though, when he didn't come home, my ears strained for the sounds of ambulance sirens, for the knock of a somber-faced policeman, the shrilling of a phone call from the hospital.

Later, when the phone did sometimes ring in the wee hours, it was him and not the authorities. It's six-something in the morning, he's been stopped for speeding on his way to work, having left the girlfriend's house too late to make it on time legally and now his van's been impounded because of that check he bounced to the DMV that he hasn't had time to cover yet. He's stranded an hour and a half from home, can I help? I didn't jump up right away – I didn't have a car and had to call around to see who would let me borrow theirs; I had to find someone to take the kids that early, and I simply had to know where his wonderful new girlfriend was this fine day. They had shared a bed every night for weeks, but she disappeared at sunrise. He didn't hold it against her anymore than he was willing to credit my account for the extraordinary, unearned generosity I showed him that morning.

I almost had it figured out. I was his "wife" when he needed laundry done or a ride home from a police station before daylight, but I was his raving, lunatic ex the rest of the time, the one accused by one girlfriend or another of "calling here bitching, pissing and moaning." When he was under the influence of vodka or regret, I was his "best friend," his "safety net." A change of mood (like the weather, predictable only with sophisticated equipment) could reset the entire scale and I'd be baffled all over again. Maybe he had a conversion chart on a laminated card – he could've kept it in his wallet next to the condoms he carried as a symbol of his independence.

Whatever I called him to his face, he was always my "husband" in my heart and mind. I did occasionally attach the adjective "estranged," delighting in its similarities to "deranged."

Sometimes the phone rang and it was one of the women. Only one was brave enough to call my house for him – and she patched a third person on to her line so she wouldn't have to ask for him herself. The woman was in Hawaii, her male friend in Australia, adding a certain exotic international flavor to my nightmare. Usually, the women called to talk to me: Did I know where he was? Did I know he stole her favorite negligee? Could I tell her how to know when he was lying?

Half-awake, I mumbled, "Are his lips moving?" I found her satin cami mixed in with my own long-abandoned lingerie. "Is it white? You can pick it up this afternoon." I said, "I have no idea where he is," even when he was passed out on my sofa bed. In those moments, I understood the thrilling power of a secret kept; I was the other woman in my own marriage.

--◆--

When I was nine, I fell from near the top of an apple tree, bouncing off the branches on the way down, knocking loose unripe apples and bits of bark, and finally, slamming hard on my back against the ground. The landing knocked the wind of out me; the panic pushed out what little usable air may have been left in my lungs. In the seconds after I hit, it felt as if something inside was broken, that irreparable damage had been done.

Those seconds of breathless panic, of pain both felt and anticipated, came back to me again in the years when hardly a day passed without the discovery of a new betrayal. Even now, when years stand between me and the revelations that left me paralyzed on the ground, gasping for breath, the mention, the thought of those days causes a physical reaction – my tongue feels thick and heavy, my stomach rolls, the breath comes only with effort.

It has been three years or so since he slept with anyone else – a statement that never feels complete without the qualifier "that I know of." I have stopped expecting to find the perfume of another woman on his skin – Imari or Sunflowers or the more intimate scents that get left behind. Still, if I were to nuzzle in and find something unfamiliar there, I wouldn't be surprised. Even now, though, some part of me might be left that could be devastated that it had happened again.

I remember an episode of *Oprah* years ago where the expert of the moment opined that there are only two emotions – love and fear. Hate, and everything else that's not love – jealousy, anger, envy, greed – are variations on the theme of fear. The theory has its merit, but it's foolish to think that love and fear are mutually exclusive, that one can't exist in the presence of the other. In an ideal world, maybe, but in the trenches of real life, fear and love are hopelessly intertwined.

"Love is a choice you make every day, with every word and action. Please let me remember that in real life and not only here on the page," read a journal entry I scribbled one bleary-eyed night. After nights like that one, fear and anger, not love, often won the day.

Having been swept away by rage, I wonder why more murders aren't committed. Crimes of passion, they're called. But it felt white-hot and overwhelming – passion can make you more aware of the world; rage obliterates everything but itself. I threw a six-foot long 2x6 at his head, having busted down the bedroom door he'd locked himself behind. He had shut himself in as a noble gesture – to protect us from each other, and from ourselves. But I couldn't allow him the honor of that – the time for honor, for upright behavior, for morals, had long since passed.

Betrayal is in the eye of the beholder. The betrayer is necessarily not objective. The sinner can't be expected to fairly assess the costs of his sins. We wish we'd done less damage. We see only what we can bear to see.

Still. I got fat. I spent too much money or lied about the money I spent, about what was paid or what wasn't. I didn't match his socks or do the housework to his standards. I can explain – I was clinically depressed; I was trying to protect him from our financial worries; I was overwhelmed with four children under six.

He was unfaithful with a co-worker of his. With my best friend. With my own sister. With a one-night stand that blossomed into a month-long affair. With a woman he met on the Internet, but never in person. He moved out and back in and out and back in and out...He never explained. He never came crawling back. Sometimes that seems the worst part of all, the least forgivable.

Sometimes though, it's one of the things that makes forgiveness possible. No excuses, no deluge of false promises. Just him, being who he is. Take it or leave it. There is a comfort in knowing you can survive the worst a person has to offer.

—◆—

What faith I have in a Supreme Being is supported almost entirely by things that have happened between us when we were unclothed. Sometimes, when we are in a bed, a moment of utter rightness happens – and in that perfect fit, I discover not only our strength but the truth of his greatest weakness. How could he ever think he belongs anywhere else? I've made the mistake of whispering that question out loud only once. I got the chuckle – sympathetic, but pushing back annoyance – and the implied, but not stated, "Every lock has its key, but some keys fit all locks."

For whole stretches of time, our sexual compatibility has been our saving grace. Even when everything else was on the verge of collapse or already round that bend, we had that fit – of bodies, desires, appetites – that seemed a blessing, a reason to keep pushing ahead. A reason at least as valid as staying together "for the sake of the children."

But for whole other stretches of time, it was the evil temptation that dragged us back into the mire. Me, because I despaired of ever finding that fit with anyone else (and I lacked inclination and courage to try); him, because despite his assertions about keys and locks, a few minutes alone in my presence was all it took to remind him of the power of the familiar. His commitment to the woman of the moment, month or year would hold up only as long as he wasn't close enough to me to touch me, smell me or remember us. Whatever his living conditions and ostensible relationships to the women in question, we never lasted longer than three months without giving in to that pull.

Every time we caved, its hold on us grew. We are together now, in part, because I have outlasted everyone else. It's part of the story he tells himself that I asked him to come back this last time, but I did not, and it has made all the difference in the balance of power – or so goes the story I tell myself.

⸻◈⸻

My marriage has lately seemed to me a stray animal, always at my heels. Not the irresistibly fluffy and perfect puppy or kitten you can dote upon and have some hope of properly training. My marriage is more a ratty German Shepherd sporting a pronounced limp, cloudy eyes, and matted patches that might be mange; so starved for affection that he salivates with gratitude when patted on the head. Whatever affection you might learn to feel for such an animal will always be tempered by an element of pity.

A friend has tried to help me define what is going on in my marriage. "Do you love him or is it just force of habit?" It's not so much force of habit as failure of imagination, maybe. I can't imagine the shape of my life without him in it. It's not a matter of soul mates or meant-to-be, imagining I could never be with anyone but him. I can only be with him because he is the one I've been with – it speaks more to coincidence than to Fate or even compatibility. I can't imagine my life without him not because of who he is but because of who I am.

"Maybe," the helpful friend presses on, "you love him, but you're not 'in love' with him." I have heard it from him: "I love you, but I'm not 'in love' with you." I grit my teeth when I hear someone making that distinction. Our societal obsession with quantifying the varieties of love, valuing one over the other strikes me as bogus and false – a phrase I picked up, by the way, from one of the girlfriends who used it in reference to his constant guitar playing. "In love" is a chemical reaction and "love" is an action you take every day. To value the one that happens to you rather than the one you make happen is not only to abdicate responsibility in your relationship but to give up control and choice in your own life.

It is love that makes forgiveness possible. What else can it be? Fear? Isn't there more to fear in this relationship than outside of it? It is love that makes me crave all that's good in him and love that feeds the hope that keeps us both in this day after day, despite the doubts that lurk at the edges of our lives. Love makes it all possible.

What makes love possible? He is home to me.

176

Reluctant Suicide
from *Saving Face*
Ron Savage

Summer, 1812 – Events of my nineteenth year

To whom it may concern: This return from the grave has given me a bad case of the vapors, and I am fainting at the most inopportune moments. I'm not sure how long I was lying on the laboratory table when I heard the professor tell his assistants, "I've changed my mind. I won't give the bastard what he wants. My *own* creation actually threatened me; said he'd harm my family if I didn't get him a bride. Can you imagine *two* of these beasts? They'd be copulating all over the damn countryside. If he must have a wife, let it be between him and the woman he finds."

You have to admire the professor. His technique has improved since putting together the creature in question – the hideous Mr. Number One – and thank you, Jesus, for that. The beast of beasts, Mr. Number One, looks like a nightmare with feet. Sewing is obviously not the professor's specialty. The stitches about the wrists, upper thigh, and neck of my would-be groom seem to go every which way. I, on the other hand, have all my parts. Your limbs don't drop off when you get diphtheria. It's the wretched disease's only virtue.

At first I feel immense relief. *Praise the Lord, praise His good name – and, please, just get me back to the grave.* Mr. Number One is *not* what anyone in her right mind would call "husband material." I mean, there's ugly and angry, then there's Mr. Number One.

Now the professor breathes an audible sigh before saying: "We might as well dispose of her."

"Do...what?" The young assistant physician is completely bewildered.

"Kill it," says the professor, meaning me.

"That would be murder," says the second assistant.

"It was al*ready* dead."

The first assistant mutters a few words under his breath. Exasperated, the professor says: "Oh, *do* speak up, Clayton."

"...It's not dead now."

---◆---

I've never been the horseback riding type; never will, particularly when I'm bound in burlap and rope, my bruised stomach bouncing on the animal's hindquarters. Though I can't see through the thick material, I hear birds and feel patches of shade and warm sunlight, and I know we're in the woods. My twin sister, Florence the Wicked, and I probably picnicked close by, that was always one of our favorite things to do on a summer afternoon. We'd drink wine and read poetry, especially Byron.

At seventeen, sister decided to live in London with my father's cousin and his wife. Though she's only a few miles away, I've never had the urge to visit, nor has she visited me. I'm ashamed to say it, but I don't miss Florence. My sister's a selfish, moody person with a talent for petty cruelties. I hear she married, the fall of last year. He's from a wealthy family.

The two assistant physicians are talking now.

The one named Clayton says, "I can't do it. I can't just kill this woman because she's suddenly become a bad idea. My God, Devon, we're physicians, *not* assassins. This sort of business goes against the grain."

"Easy for you to be generous," says Devon. "This research job with the professor pays my tuition. Most of us don't have your money."

"Then *you* kill her."

Both of them stay quiet for awhile. The only sounds are the distant birds and the clopping hooves of their horses on stone and earth.

Finally, Devon said: "We could leave her here. You know, take her deeper into the woods and simply leave her."

"Let God decide?"

"Vengeance *is* His, isn't it?"

Then I feel the rope snapping loose about my calves and arms.

Clayton whispers, "It's the best I can do."

Later and alone, I stare into a pond, see my face, and scream. *My dear, sweet Lord, what did that horrid professor do to me?* I have *no* face. Yet I'm sure I was buried with one. I see only its underbelly, the bones and muscle, the dried crusted blood. I start screaming, again. Along with all the shrieking, I decide to run through the forest like a crazy person. Eventually, though, I hide myself in a nearby cave. No sense scaring the children.

I'm trying to remember what happened to me, but my mind isn't cooperating. Thoughts have been replaced by a splendid vacuousness, and I can't recall diddly-squat, as Florence liked to say. Then it simply occurs: *Oh, Jesus, I was being electrocuted.*

The professor had put something metal on my head and feet. I recall waking up to flashes of light, to sparks that exploded outward like fireworks, and to the smell of burning flesh...my face. I could see the flames leaping off my cheeks, my mouth and chin. This was how he'd brought me back from the dead, this bastard, this heathen, this heartless vicious demon who's obviously no different than Mr. Number One.

Clayton visits me every night. There's something familiar about him, incredibly familiar, almost a *déjà vu* experience. Waiting eagerly to hear the clip-clop sound of his horse outside the cave, I find myself combing out what hair I have with cracked and dirty fingernails.

Tonight, though, he seems different, more remote and anxious. I immediately think he wants to stop our visits but doesn't know how to say this without hurting my feelings. When he does finally speak, I'm startled into silence.

He says he married my sister Florence.

My God, I remember him. Who in her right mind forgets a first love?

He squints at me, trying to glimpse past the shadows in the cave, but my face isn't the sort to give away hints. As if apologizing for his choice in wives, he says the marriage has never gone well. Among her many cruelties, she cheats on him, typical of Florence. Two weeks ago her recent lover attempted to kill Clayton with a straight razor.

Maybe it's remembering the love we'd felt for each other as children – the love I've grown to feel for him now – or the horror of this so-called life – perhaps both, I don't know – but I start to weep, just uncontrollable sobs. He takes my hand, holds it for a moment, and kisses it.

"Don't go worrying yourself," Clayton says, and brushes his lips over my fingers again. "I've been working on a plan for us...for you."

He retrieves sandals and a brown hooded monk's robe from his saddlebag. I eat supper quickly and put on my cleric disguise.

Clayton helps me onto the back of his horse. Before clicking his heels into the animal's sides, he says I should hold him tightly. We're going to the professor's laboratory to fix my face. Then he says he has always loved me.

I've forgotten the enormity of the room. Its wood floor and walls are bathed in moonlight that enters through a series of small windows high above us. Before me are three metal tables, the middle one empty. Mr. Number One is stretched out on the table to the right – he's asleep, perhaps drugged, I don't know – and to the left, a smaller body hidden by a canvas tarp.

"Drink this," Clayton says, and hands me a glass vial containing a pale orange liquid. "You need to sleep while I mend your face."

He explains that the medicine is a sedative, but it will also help my body accept the new skin and remove any scars caused by the surgery. Then Clayton says something cryptic: "You can thank the beast for this," he says. When I glance over to Mr. Number One, I notice the thing has lost its own scars, not a single mark on its wrists, its neck. The thought of having a new face is so wondrous, so sublime, that I swallow the pale orange liquid without hesitation. After all, if I can't trust Clayton, who can I trust in this terrible life?

My dearest Clayton, you will always be my "to whom it may concern." I cannot begin to describe the blessing of our last 33 years together. But you and I both know the danger waiting for you and the children. Though I don't discuss it, the dreams *are* getting worse, and the violence is more than I can bear...or can now control. The article in yesterday's *Times*, the one about the zoo and the dead animals, how they were so horribly mutilated, I'm sure I had something to do with that. Occasionally, we must sacrifice ourselves to protect others.

Remember what you told me all those years ago? "You can thank the beast for this," you said. Our night in the laboratory, before the sedative took hold, I saw the orange liquid draining from the back of Mr. Number One's head into a small brass bowl on the wood floor. I saw what was under that canvas tarp, too. You must love me very much, my darling. Thank you for my beautiful face – such a perfect fit – and there's not a scar anywhere on my body.

I also hope you've been proven right and Mr. Number One has finally found his bride. Such a simpatico ending. I wonder if she's happy.

Under My Eaves
Susan Baller-Shepard

It hangs heavy outside my window
the icy drops form a spear
that blocks the sunlight coming in
for the skies are gray for days
and it does not melt.

Who knows
when the icicle plummets –
all the ways I described it,
like glass, like crystal, like something of God
all of that for naught
as it slides from my eaves
to shatter on cement below.

I learn something of the hardness
of things, as I watch the ice break.
Life deals you things that break irreparably.
You meet people you love, and the answer
is "not now," or maybe it's "no," or maybe "never."
That everything melts and breaks loose.
Including you.
Especially you.

182

New Moon
Margie Shelly

Tonight the moon hangs differently; I am on top of you, giving you roses,
feeling the soft curve of your body slipping away from me
as velvet does before touch.

I reach for your breast,
discover the pale white of your skin.
The one light in the room marks you in fine detail.

Now I know that to enter you I must be a magician with a bag of tricks,
pull your hair gently away from the sides of your head
to smell the pale flower of winter.

Now I feel my entering of you:
Soft rhythms live inside you as you begin to speak
a word you never finish.

If I am on top, will I feel the gravitational pull to you?
If I am in charge, will I see your eyes as two pools of thought
entering my bloodstream, quickening the pace of my heart?

One light on in this room, a certain transmittal of volts.
One face in this room with transparent eyes.
One moon outside hanging thinly, hanging surely.

If I am you, I must learn to speak a new language
Resonating of flesh that is given, whispering when it is received.
If I am you, I must speak with purpose
and the purpose is to have this new moon
be fresh, be thin, be bright enough to allow a proposition:
I must birth magic, be both man and woman.

184

Will This Circle Be Unbroken?
Grazina Smith

> Will the circle be unbroken
> By and by, Lord, by and by
> There's a better home a waitin'
> In the sky, Lord, in the sky
> – Anon.

The line between the world I know and the unseen world around me seems very thin, as if my peripheral vision is too poor and I can't turn my head fast enough to come face-to-face with that other world. I come by this understanding naturally, descending from Lithuanian ancestors who worshiped Spirits long after most of Europe was Christian. Perkunas, the mighty Thunder God, is still acknowledged in Lithuania's public places with restaurant names, statues in parks and his ruined altars underneath our great cathedrals. It is as if the ancient religion ripples like a gentle undertow to our Christianity.

185

My grandmother personified the richness of that dual tradition. She was named Laima after the Goddess of Fate. She had a sixth sense and was aware of the world hovering beyond her reach. Trees were sacred to her and a fragrant pine grew near her cottage. Laima lived by the sea and as a child, I spent my summers with her, often sitting in the shade of that tree. She encouraged me to slip off my sandals and plant my feet on the soil to feel the power of Mother Earth. She said trees united the heavens, the earth and the underworld. From their roots sprang life and wisdom, from their trunks, strength, and their branches caressed the sky.

Laima mixed our Christian religion with ancient ancestral beliefs. She took me to Sunday Mass and we said prayers every morning, but our summers were also filled with daily rituals to appease the Spirits. We left milk outside for minor deities who inhabited the forests. At night, we sang songs to the Star God as he threw his net across the sky. Grandmother had a Rugiu Boba (Rye Woman) hanging on the wall. The doll was woven from rye cut from her brother's fields, and by honoring her, we assured a plentiful harvest the following year.

It hung next to the palms blessed on Palm Sunday which Laima twisted into an ornate cross and studded with dry wild flowers. Even our berry picking in the woods started with a chant and an offering of the first ripe berries to the Moss God. (*Samanelis, fill my basket with sweet berries...*)

My grandmother understood we couldn't enter into the unseen world but she also knew spirits crossed that boundary often and meddled in men's affairs. Most fervently, she believed my grandfather, Saulius (named after the Sun Goddess) watched over her every day of her life – not as a dreamy, looking-down-from-the-sky abstraction but really there in a parallel existence. He died when my mother was a child and grandmother kept lighted candles before the one photo she had taken by an itinerant photographer on their wedding day. She whispered to him during the day and at night, she smoothed the pillow next to her, sleeping on half the bed to leave room for him when he came to rest.

As I grew older I thought her devotion strange and felt uncomfortable when she talked about him as if he had only gone for a day's fishing on the Baltic Sea. During one summer trip to her cottage, I complained to my parents.

"She has an imaginary husband." I said. My father laughed.

"Your grandmother plans to remain faithful to Saulius 'until we meet beyond the sunset,' as she puts it."

"Your grandmother loves you very much," my mother chimed in, defending her side of the family. "And she will not forget your grandfather as long as she lives."

Not forgetting him is one thing, I thought, *but talking to his spirit – that is another.*

I didn't have the nerve to say that out loud, but my mother could read my face and, in bits and pieces, she eventually told me their unusual love story.

❖

According to unwritten rules of country life, Laima and Saulius should never have met. People stayed close to their villages in those days – not traveling even 20 kilometers from their birthplaces. Laima's father was a farmer and she lived far from the Sea. Saulius was a fisherman who plied his trade on the Baltic. She said it was fate that brought them together. Perhaps, but fate took the form of Henrikas, the wealthy old landlord whose estate was near the fishing village. Henrikas trusted Saulius and hired him to go to the city and bring back a stallion he had purchased. The horse was shipped from Poland and Saulius, curious about city life, agreed to the journey. It took him

10 days, and on the way back, he rode through the village where Laima lived. She was weeding the flower beds in front of her parent's cottage when he saw her and later claimed her face was the reason God gave him sight.

Laima often told me about that day. When a shadow covered her flowers, she looked up and saw a handsome man standing by the gate staring at her. He was leading a magnificent white stallion and, for a moment, she thought he was a prince who had stepped out of a fairy tale. She never told me what they talked about but Saulius returned three more times, borrowing a work horse from Henrikas to make the journey. On the fourth trip, he hitched the horse to a cart, decorated both of them with garlands of wild flowers, and came to take her back with him. Laima packed her few belongings into her dowry chest. She did not heed her mother's weeping for future grandchildren who would live too far away or listen to her father's pleas to wait until he learned more about the man she planned to marry.

"I wasn't hard-hearted," Laima reminisced, "and it made me sad to leave them but I knew there was no other man for me but Saulius."

Happiness wove their lives together and each day seemed better than the last until, a year after their marriage, my mother was born.

"We were blessed to have our baby," Laima said. "The only time I saw my husband's eyes fill with tears was when he first held Ona." Life settled into a joyous pattern. Laima tended her daughter, her house and her garden; Saulius caught the fish they ate and the eels they smoked to sell at city markets. But happiness seldom continues uninterrupted, and after they had been married for three years, the fish disappeared from the sea. Even going far from shore, fishermen returned with empty nets. The joy Saulius felt in his family turned to anxiety as he worried how he would provide for them. Finally, he went to Henrikas and asked for a loan to purchase food through the winter. Saulius insisted on an official paper for the loan and made his mark on a promissory note.

It was a harsh winter and, during it, Henrikas died. His son, Petras, inherited the estate. Henrikas had been a generous landlord. He allowed the villagers to gather firewood from his forests, to trap small game and cut logs for boat repairs. He hung a pair of fine black leather boots on a clothesline in the kitchen and any groom could borrow them for his wedding instead of wearing wooden clogs on such an important day.

Petras had spent most of his life in the city and treated the fishermen with contempt, believing them to be foolish and superstitious. His carriage raced through the village, scattering children and killing any geese in the way. He forbade anyone to enter his forest and the wedding boots could only be used in exchange for a week's labor. The fishermen cursed him among themselves.

"The devil take him! He'd flay the skin off our backs and laugh as he did it."

That spring, the fish began to slowly return and Saulius worked long hours to increase his catch and repay his loan. Petras now held the promissory note and my grandfather wanted to pay off his debt quickly. He began to fish further and further from shore hoping to catch the eels prized in the city.

When my grandmother talked of her husband's death, she always spoke allegorically, blaming Jurate, the Sea Goddess, for not allowing him to return.

"Jurate was very jealous of our happiness," she said. "She decided to keep Saulius in her undersea palace and won't let him come back to me."

She regaled me with stories of a shimmering amber palace, ruled by a mermaid goddess who controlled every fish, every drop of water and forced Saulius to stay with her. After summer storms, Laima took me to the shore and we searched for amber chunks washed up on the sand. When we found one, she whispered,

"Look, your grandfather broke off a bit of the palace for you. We'll polish it and you'll see how it glows."

My mother's story of her father's death was brutally honest.

"My father drowned," she would say. "I was young but remember it clearly. The fishermen returned at noon, and when Papa didn't return with them, we went to the shore. The men said they saw him take his boat further out to sea. 'Don't worry,' they told Mama. 'The sea is calm. He'll be back.' We stood on the beach all day and all night. The sky stayed pewter gray, never getting totally dark, and a heavy mist rose from the sea. I couldn't tell where the earth ended and the heavens began. The damp made me shiver and I wrapped myself in Mama's long red, woolen skirt and sat by her feet. Mama never moved. She stared at the horizon as if the strength of her will could make that small boat appear. The men finally dragged her away the next morning. I guess they took pity on me, whimpering, hungry and cold. We never found his body and Mama wore black from that day."

"No wonder she thinks he's a prisoner in a palace under the sea," I whispered.

"Worse was to come," my mother continued. "She was alone and had to feed me. The fishing was poor that year; her neighbors struggled to feed themselves. She thought about returning to her parents, but it was too painful to leave the cottage where she had known such happiness. She began to trespass into the forest to gather nuts, mushrooms, berries and that's where Petras first saw her. The next day, he stopped his carriage and came to her door with the promissory note. 'This loan is overdue and must be paid.' He looked around our cottage. 'Why do you live in this hovel?' he asked. 'Come to the Manor and live under my protection.' He returned to cajole her every day. She shook her head and didn't answer, thinking he would tire of this game. Others knew it would end badly."

My mother never clearly explained why living in the Manor was unacceptable and, when I was a child, it seemed very mysterious. She only said men like Petras were controlled by their arrogance and desires, which burned hot and reckless, consuming everything in their way.

It all ended on the coldest winter night in memory. It was just past Christmas and the Manor was filled with guests, feasting and drinking. Petras had invited my grandmother to join them. In the middle of the merriment, he demanded his sleigh and rode out – dressed in all his finery, the sleigh shining with silver trappings, pulled by a troika of two black horses with the white stallion in the lead. Petras burst into Liama's cottage.

189

"Why didn't you come?" He spoke softly, sorrowfully, as if regretting the action he would take. "I've waited long enough and must have this hovel in payment of the loan. My men will be here to set you out in the morning. It's up to you where you go – but you're welcome to come to the Manor"

When Laima looked at him coldly, her mouth set in a tight line, he continued.

"You're a foolish and stubborn woman. I offer you a much better life. What have you here?" He asked. "There's no one to help you but me." He shook his head and left the cottage.

Laima ran to the window and saw the white stallion pawing the ground. After the sleigh left, she began keening. Her voice rose as she called out to Saulius.

"How could you leave me?" She wailed. "What have you done? Henrikas never wanted a note. Your pride made you sign it."

Her cries filled the room and my mother hid under the bed covers. They both wept that night, holding on to each other. At daybreak, there was a pounding at the door and Laima expected to be evicted. When she answered the door, the villagers told her of a miracle.

A fisherman had been furtively gathering firewood in the forest when he heard sleigh bells. He peered through the trees and saw Petras gliding over the frozen sea. When the sleigh was far from shore, a great light rose from the bottom, scintillating through the ice, illuminating the sleigh until it dazzled. The merry jingle of sleigh bells was overpowered by a rumbling, like Thunder, and a sharp crack as the ice crust broke. A jagged split appeared and the heavy sleigh sank through the gap into the frigid water.

When Laima heard this, she only said, "It's a shame to lose such fine horses."

The next morning, men went out on the lake, but found no signs of a break in the ice. The snow lay smooth as if a sleigh had never crossed it. After the spring thaw, flashes of light danced on the water as sun struck the sleigh's silver trappings. The fishermen avoided that area even though the fattest eels could be found there. Having often cursed Petras, they believed the devil finally took him, but Laima knew it was Saulius who saved her. She trusted him to care for her from that day.

I have a few of my grandmother's things – her wooden dowry chest, eight lumpy nuggets of amber and her sepia-colored wedding photo. Her husband's arm is draped around her waist, his feet encased in shiny, borrowed boots. But her legacy is much more than these things. Laima taught me to believe in the process of life, the strength of love, and the healing power of nature. Often, I find myself stopping to stare at a magnificent tree, itching to take off my shoes and feel the earth. In those quiet moments, Laima shimmers just out of reach, watching me and I know love is eternal. Like a raindrop that falls into the ocean, love draws its power from the whole, uniting our past and our future, allowing us to love again and again.

Summer Storm
Beverly Sweet

it is an awful fight
you rage for hours on end
I weep like sky ripped open

the dog hides from the noise
you smoke too many cigarettes
I lock myself in the car

twenty minutes later I drive away

lightning flashes over the bay
a heat storm on the cusp of a new moon

when I return home
we sit on the pier
hold hands
drink wine

watch silver fire blaze

192

Who by Fire (excerpt)
Mary L. Tabor

The Fire: If I could have, I would have told Lila about the fire I saw in Iowa, but it is regret that writes this, that longs for said things unsaid.

This fire would have amazed her. The heat was so incredibly hot that it reminded me of something I learned in physics: the fact that the air around a lightning bolt is hotter than the surface of the sun. It was a barn burning – not with any political or racial overtones, but a necessary burn of an old wooden grain bin in the center of town in Whiting, Iowa, where I grew up. She was a Baltimore-grown city girl who wouldn't be able to imagine this story of the burning, though I suppose it's a common enough event in rural parts of our country.

That I know something Lila couldn't imagine amazes me.

The year before she died, she gave me the scores for Beethoven's *Piano Concerto No. 5 in E-flat Major*, the "Emperor"; for Mahler's *Symphony No. 1 in D Major*, the "Titan"; for Schubert's *Piano Quintet in A Major, D667*, the "Trout"; and for Stravinsky's "The Firebird." She gave me these books with their multiple staffs of notes – "The Firebird" with notes for two piccolos, two flutes, two oboes, an English horn, three clarinets, a bass clarinet, three bassoons, three trombones, a tuba, violins, the piano and many others – when I was no longer playing the piano that sat in our living room, an old black Steinway baby grand that I hadn't tuned in over a year. How could I play a piano out of tune? I didn't tune it to ensure I wouldn't play, wouldn't be jarred by the notes ringing wrong against my ear, pitching awkwardly, ironically, accusing me.

The piano lay quiet like the word piano but sat there hard, visible, concrete. Like Isaac – Isaac was Lila's lover – like Isaac, who leaves his dried-up watercolors in his potting shed and wants minimalism, wants geometry, the thing that insists on being only itself, I left my piano to sit like a minimalist statement. Like Isaac who had stopped painting, I knew I could never play well enough to satisfy. No matter how good my touch, my sense of pitch, it was never good enough.

193

When I played the piano, I heard all the possible interpretations of the phrasing, the tones, versus what I was able to produce from the sounding board. My inability to reproduce those interpretations, no matter how well I did play, accused me—the reason I stopped.

Lila told me that the revered Rabbi Akiva had 24,000 disciples who studied his teachings and came up with 24,000 interpretations. She found this comforting and would repeat it to counter my certainty that I couldn't play.

I hold the scores of music, listen to the sounds of the instruments, 28 different ones in "The Firebird," blending with one another, and can hear each one in its staff of music on the page. I don't see the fabulous bird with its plumage of fire. I don't see the ballerina who goes on point and is lifted in flight. I have heard of but not seen Chagall's designs for the sets. I have never seen Balanchine's choreography of this music. In the quiet, the score in my hand, I don't need to put a CD in my player. In "The Princesses' Round: Khorovode," I hear a lullaby, lean back to let the flutist know that he should play his low notes, that the oboe's haunting tones should enter.

I hear what I conduct.

She understood this would happen. It was her gift. In return I didn't play the piano. I didn't read the scores in front of her. I didn't let her see my hands fly through the air, the score in my lap held open by a slide rule.

I was like a cold burn.

In Whiting, when I was a child, the house across the street blew up in a silent explosion while I slept. Bake, who lived there with his wife and children, had gone down to the basement before five in the morning because the house was cold. Our guess is that he lit a match to light the boiler and the air exploded around him, throwing him onto the floor with a head injury that would kill him, while his wife and children ran from the house before its walls fell in on themselves. The firemen came to put out a fire that hadn't occurred and I woke to the single siren of the town's one fire truck. This explosion that made no sound any of us heard – who knows what Bake heard before he fell? – was a cold burn, is how I think of it.

In "The Infernal Dance Of King Katscheï," I let the horns dominate the strings and recall the siren that woke me when I was a child and think how Lila waited for me. But I was a silent explosion. She hoped I'd break through and come to her, burst on her with desire from joy, from playing the piano, where she saw that could happen. She must have believed that's what she got from Isaac. I don't know what he felt for her though I try. I have begun to know what she felt for him because I understand what she couldn't get from me.

I've hated him, have tried to imagine I was the cool center between them – the space that kept them apart.

When I was a child, I put out a candle flame with my fingers. A trick. I thought the blue place in the center was cold. "Is it?" I asked my father. He said, "No," said something about oxygen – its presence, its absence – "air," he said. Breath, I think now. He said, "It does seem impossible, doesn't it? No burn?" We looked at my fingers. He said, "Consider it a paradox."

I know now that the hottest part of the flame is just above the blue core, that temperatures vary inside the flame. I stare into a fire, the blue light, the gold fire, the smoke that engulfs the glint of blue, what I once saw as "cold" fire.

Isaac and Lila's embrace combusted fast despite the lost time that had separated them. They came to that point in time slowly, through knowing and not knowing one another, through space and time, as if they'd had a time of cold fire. Her time with me, perhaps?

The poet Frost (forgive the pun on cold-fire, unintentional), who said, "From what I've tasted of desire/ I hold with those who favor fire," in a masculine rhymed couplet and perfect meter that I find annoying, also said in rhythmic variation that suits my sense of sound, "All is an interminable chain of longing."

You might observe that I, her husband, am an ordinary cuckold, mocked by their longing, that I am an old story you already know, that I am angry, want revenge and so I write to expose them. But you would be wrong.

I have become, instead of angry, full of self-loathing. The idea of just or unjust desserts, either conclusion, now comes too easy. Her death has made former conclusions mere notions.

Lila's mother loved the "Notions Department" at the May Company, where she worked when she was a young woman, where she went when she was a housewife and a seamstress. She bought thread there, the seam ripper that she treasured with its curved, sharp end for pulling out thread tightly sewn and that she used for the seam in need of letting out or taking in, in need of an adjustment.

These small necessities, the notions, are part and parcel of making the garment that we call life and that death rips asunder.

I've begun with a notion: the fire I saw in Iowa because it was a direct hit for me. Leonard Bernstein said about music, "It doesn't have to pass through the censor of the brain before it can reach the heart ...

An F-sharp doesn't have to be considered in the mind; it is a direct hit." The fire was like that for me and thus has become what may seem to you an obsession. And so it is.

I stood with my father in the center of town in Whiting, Iowa, after the burn in the heat of the fire, recalled the flame I put out with my fingers as a child, stood with him in the cool of the summer night under a sky after fire.

I think of Lila this way: sky after fire.

If you'd asked me to name the color of the fire when I began this, I would have said, "Red" because I liked to think of myself as a simple man, prided myself on my lack of spontaneity. Now I think of the blue inside or even of some other color: green fire, black fire, white fire.

How You Love
Keith Vanden Eynden

David paced the sidewalk in front of the courthouse, drawing stares from the passersby. A stream of tourists in brightly colored shorts, tank tops, and T-shirts eyed him as he adjusted his cummerbund and nervously scanned the street. Heat rose off the asphalt, burning away the thick mist that smudged the hard lines between the buildings.

It reminded him of early mornings at Kings Island before the patrons arrived, when dew hung on the blades of Kentucky bluegrass and soaked his canvas sneakers. The sunlight reflected back from acres of blacktop promised the sweltering freedom of summer – something like the anticipation he felt now.

Walking across International Street before the amusement park opened, David regarded the complicated crosshatched beams of the replica Eiffel Tower. He drank in the emptiness and the surge of fountains in the center of the avenue. As the day wore on, the crowds would transform his solitude into loneliness, soiling what felt so natural now. Cloaked in this peace, he almost reconsidered his plans.

He passed through the different themed areas: Old Coney, with its turn-of-the-century games and roller coasters; River Town, echoing with the gunshots of the Old West and the raging water of log flumes. The Congo, David's area, thrummed with bongos and African chants.

He shuffled away from the center of the park to the fringes, with his royal blue windbreaker wrapped around him, losing himself in the fricative rhythm of his cuffs. The sound of his footsteps became hollow as he left the path and crossed the bridge that separated the Congo from the rest of the park. Unlike the symmetrical order of the other buildings, his shop, Congo Curio, with faux thatch roof and grass walls, presented indistinct, blurry borders.

As David pulled the door open, he rehearsed his speech under his breath, trying to sound natural. *Maybe...if you weren't doing anything...Maybe you might want to see a movie with me. Maybe we could see* Mask.

Though he'd only seen the trailers, David knew he wanted a mother like Rusty Dennis had in that movie, a mother who loved her son despite his Lionitis, a disease which made his face resemble a malformed potato. Rusty bullied her son into believing that he had nothing to be ashamed of, while David's mother found his unseen defects and dragged them into the light – his struggle to make friends, his withdrawn nature, and his lack of a girlfriend.

"How about Gretchen?" his mother had asked. "At least she talks to you. Besides, I like her name. We were going to call you Gretchen if you'd been a girl."

For a chance to win her approval, he struggled to recite the words with confidence. "How about tomorrow night?"

"Morning."

David jumped, startled by the brusque voice. He hadn't expected anyone, let alone Gretchen, the girl he was rehearsing for.

With seven female employees to every one boy, Kings Island was a Catholic schoolboy's fantasy. In the Congo, David was one of only two guys. His mother surmised that even *he* should be able to get a date. But even with these odds firmly in his mind, he still wasn't ready to approach Gretchen. If she rejected him, he'd have to work with her for an entire shift, her disapproving stare a weight on his back like a tumor. Then, after work, he'd face his mother's recrimination as well.

"Jesus, look at this!" Gretchen's mouth pulled down in a scowl, her eyes narrowing.

"What?" David asked, his answer obscured by the sound of the door swinging open.

"Morning," Kelly said and blew across the shop, heading for the back.

"Look at this, David!" She gestured wildly with her arm.

Kelly mimicked Gretchen's mannerisms behind her back before shoving into the stockroom. David smiled in spite of himself.

"Did you close last night?"

"Yes," David answered, smoothing his expression.

Gretchen's long dark hair hung heavy around her face, streaked black where it was still wet. From several feet away, he could smell her shampoo, her powder deodorant, and he felt nauseous.

"Look at this plush." Gretchen motioned toward the shelves of stuffed animals behind her. They leaned drunkenly against each other, a pointillistic collage of bears, flamingos, and dinosaurs.

"Looks like a Technicolor yawn," Kelly said, exiting the storeroom and punting a rogue parrot across the tile floor.

"It looks like shit. I've told you to straighten this stuff up before you leave. There's only one register open after 9:00. There's no reason you can't clean up before we close."

"I didn't work last night. I went to the movies," Kelly said. "I saw *Mask*. It was great – about this disfigured boy. You'd really identify with him, Gretchen. I was sitting in the dark saying to myself – "

"I wasn't talking to you. I was talking to him." David was laughing now. Gretchen glared at him, but he couldn't stop. "I'm going to open Kilimanjaro. Have this cleaned up before I get back." The door scraped and slammed.

David knelt on the floor and was segregating the animals before he realized he had blown his chance with Gretchen. And yet his body relaxed, the awkward script dissolving into a vague mist.

"Have you seen it yet?" Kelly pitched the wayward parrot onto the top shelf.

"What?"

"*Mask*."

"No," David answered. "But I want to."

"We should see it together."

"But you've already seen it."

"That's okay. It was good enough to see again."

"Well, I was actually going to ask Gretchen to see it with me."

Kelly suppressed a laugh. "Do you really think that's going to happen?"

David matched Kelly's smile. "No." He took a deep breath. It coasted down his throat unrestricted, without hesitation, like a tethered spirit returning home. "Okay. When should we go?" Nothing in his life felt as natural as that question.

David claimed he would have never picked Kelly. He once said, "It must be true love because I've always been attracted to brunettes." Kelly's hair was sun-streaked, nearly white. If he'd followed his preference for brunettes, where would that have led him? To a life with Gretchen? A dismal life pretending at love?

He couldn't explain his attraction to Kelly to his mother, either.

"What happened to Gretchen?" she'd asked that night. "I thought you were going to ask Gretchen out. What about her?"

What about her? David thought as he scanned the thickening crowd of people for Kelly. In the 19 years since that day, he'd often imagined

Gretchen divorced several times, ambling through an empty two-story house, confused about why her marriages kept failing. It was mean-spirited, but he felt that her ruined love life – even a ruined love life that only existed in his head – legitimized his accomplishment.

More people like him coursed up the walk now: men and women in wedding attire, expectant and nervous. Then he saw Kelly buoyed up by the flow, wearing that smile. Without a word they met, grasped hands, and raced to the courthouse, taking the stairs two at a time.

In the foyer, clumps of brides and grooms wandered directionless, many crying, some shaking their heads. Voices echoed off the rotunda, peppered with strained tones. David and Kelly approached the desk. Ahead of them, two women wearing tuxedoes confronted the receptionist, and David's heart fell.

"I'm sorry, ladies. The Supreme Court told us to stop." The gangly, unkempt official raised his arms and projected his voice so he'd only have to make the announcement once, obviously anxious to return to the dark anonymity of his office.

David clutched Kelly's hand and looked into his clear blue eyes. "You couldn't have been early for once?"

"I didn't even take time to shave," Kelly replied. He tried to ignite his smile again, but it sputtered and went out.

David reached up and caressed the fine blond stubble on Kelly's face, the strong cut of his jaw.

"I just thought we'd finally belong. That we'd be recognized for what we've done."

Kelly gently pulled David's hand from his chin. Clutching it, he slid the plain gold band onto his lover's finger.

Thrown
Rose Vanden Eynden

guess I didn't hear him enter. By the time I sat immersed in warm water and peaks of bubbles, he stood in the bathroom doorway, arms stretched out on either side of his lanky body, hands supporting his weight as he leaned in. In the outline of the hall lamplight, he looked like Christ on the cross. It was me, though, that felt a stab of pain, deep in my belly. Or maybe it was just the baby kicking.

"Hey," he said softly, as if trying not to spook one of his precious horses.

I turned my head away to hide my surprise by studying the mildew darkening the grout. The colors swam together, pink and black. Goddamn hormones. I cupped my hands and splashed water on my face to camouflage the tears in my eyes.

When I spoke, I sounded normal, although my whole body shook so badly the water rippled around me. "What're you doing here?"

"Still live here, last I checked." Smooth and rough, his voice, like a satin tablecloth pulled along old, splintered wood. Lucas was like that – strange contrasts, sharp corners and soft edges, a man hardened by life and sweetened by a grace I couldn't understand. He made it difficult to love him, and easy to miss him. I had missed him, spending all my lonely minutes convincing myself that I'd never loved him at all.

"Are you sure?" I tilted my head back down, my eyes on the soapy water, but I could still see him in my peripheral vision. Crystals of snow dotted the shoulders of his heavy denim jacket, and his hands were beginning to lose the red color of cold-bitten skin. He never liked wearing gloves, even when he roped and rode. I'd sat many nights in this very bathroom, swabbing his split skin from where the reins had burned his palms crimson and purple. He'd finally submitted to gloves when he'd started riding the circuit full-time, but he wouldn't wear them just because of weather.

His hands. How I wanted him to touch me, even then. I closed my eyes to keep from seeing them slipping, lifting the hem of my blouse in my memory. I slid my own palms across my stretched belly, reminding myself that there were other things between us, too.

"You're my wife, Amy." Simple, straightforward as always. I opened my eyes and stared at him, at the bowed crown of his head. His blond hair had grown longer, curling around his ears and over his brow. It hid his eyes, but I didn't need to see them. I could hear the gentle plea in his tone.

Disbelief chuffed out of me in a short breath. I slid forward in the tub and grabbed my razor from its place beside the soap dish. My left leg appeared, bubbles clinging, and came to rest on the tub rim. I raked the bar of soap along the skin above my knee. "Huh. Your wife. You should've thought of that before you left me here alone for two months."

Lucas shuffled his feet; the light bounced off the silver toes of his boots and caught my attention. My cowboy. In all my wildest dreams, I'd never imagined the life I had. A city girl, educated, with a string of doctors and lawyers as ex-es, married to a rodeo rider who'd left her high, dry, and pregnant. Ironic, how love blinds you, leaves you helpless, stupid, and inert.

202

I clutched the razor and stretched forward, straining to reach my foot, but my pregnant belly wouldn't allow it. I twisted a couple of different ways to no avail. Frustrated, I slapped the water, sloshing it over the side of the tub.

"What're you trying to do?" Calm, like a placid lake on a still morning. His ease infuriated me.

"What does it look like I'm trying to do, Lucas? I can't reach to shave my legs, goddamn it. No thanks to you."

"I can help." He shrugged off his jacket and bent to remove his boots.

"Don't bother." But he was already kneeling on the bath mat beside the tub, his face close, shadowed with stubble. His fingers closed around my fist, gently pulling the razor from me. His gaze was deep and green, like moss in an ancient, quiet forest. He hypnotized me with a soft smile as he dropped his free hand into the water.

He rubbed the cake of soap along the curve of my calf, blending it with bubbles into froth. Then he turned the razor and carefully positioned it in the notch next to my ankle, dragging it easily up my leg to the side of my knee. I gulped in a breath as he plunged the razor into the water to rinse it, his knuckles brushing my hip. Something electric sizzled where he touched me; I bit my lip to remind me of pain.

"I found her." He was rinsing the razor again when he said it, and I nearly lost his words in the splashing. The baby seemed to jump along with my heart.

"What?"

"My mother. I found her."

He didn't look at me. The razor continued to slide up my leg; Lucas navigated it along the slope with an effortless grace. His hand betrayed him, though – it shook as he guided it over my knee, nicking the skin and bringing a pinprick of blood to the surface.

My voice was a whisper of awe. "You found your mother?"

He nodded as he reached across me to the inside of my leg. I could smell him, snow and sweat, clean sweetness and sour weight, so familiar it made my throat close, aching. He swept away another trail of lather on the underside of my calf.

"She's a doctor in Montana." The razor dipped and made a tiny whirlpool as he swirled it around. "She gave me up because she couldn't be a single mother in med school."

203

"You talked to her?"

"Yeah." A sardonic smile darkened his light features. "She thought I wanted money." He finished the final swipe on my leg, his eyes following the razor as it moved. Then he set it on the rim of the tub, leaned over, and pressed his lips to my knee, to the spot where the blade had drawn blood.

I dropped my leg back into the water, choking out my reply. "You can't kiss this better, Lucas."

He sighed. "Put your other leg up here."

"No." My voice was controlled again. "I'll find another way to do it."

He stood, unfurling himself like a thrown lasso, and began unbuttoning his shirt. He peeled off one garment at a time, slowly, deliberately, watching me watch him. Then he stepped into the tub, wedging himself between my back and the cool porcelain. His body burned like hot coals as he nestled against me.

I felt his right leg nudge mine, his knee brushing the back of my thigh, bending my leg with his. Our limbs rose together from the water, mine on top, glimmering with a sheen of soapsuds. He picked up the razor.

"This OK?" His breath was humid in my ear. I nodded mutely, dizzy from his nearness. The razor made its first pass on my leg, and he cocked his head, watching his work and murmuring against my neck.

"I had to go. I've been looking for her my whole life."

"I could've gone with you. You didn't even ask me. You didn't even tell me!" My anger made me shake again, and his other arm crossed my breasts, drawing me against his chest. We trembled together, like two dried leaves on an autumn tree, waiting for the wind to blow us away.

"I had to go by myself. I had to see where I came from. What she was." His left hand broke the water's surface and rubbed the side of my abdomen. His wedding band winked like a distant headlight on a deserted road. "Before I became a father, I had to know."

I grasped his hand, the one holding the razor, and he dropped it immediately, twining his fingers through mine. "I thought you'd left me." The words hitched out of me in short bursts. "Left us. How could you do that, Lucas?"

His cheek sagged into my shoulder and his voice quavered with emotion.

"I'd never do that. Don't you understand? I know what it's like to grow up wondering. I should've told you, I guess, but..." He trailed off. Talking never came easy to Lucas, and the struggle made his voice stagger. I didn't help him, though. He had to say it, and I had to hear it.

"She's the only woman I ever knew before you. And I didn't know her. I had this dream that she'd welcome me, kiss me, sit me down to catch up over coffee. She didn't do any of that. She didn't even invite me into her house." He gathered me into his chest, clutching me to him like a buoy in a bay. "She didn't want me. Even though I'd hoped different, I couldn't take that chance – you seeing *that*."

His tears in my hair melted my dried heart, like rain soaking parched earth. I pulled his arms tighter around me, cradling our unborn child. "We want you, Lucas," I whispered. His trembling quieted. After a moment, his finger moved across the skin of my belly, tracing wetness into shorthand. A straight, perpendicular line. A tiny, lopsided heart. An upside-down horseshoe. His apology, to our child and to me.

I took his hand and brought it to my lips, kissing forgiveness into his palm. My cowboy. In the rodeo, I'd never understood how the riders could be thrown from a wild horse, get up, dust off their wounds, and jump back in the saddle.

Maybe I'm more of a cowboy than I want to admit.

Wild Aster
Claudia Van Gervan

Stars as distant
as the Pleiades bloom
on the banks of Bear Creek.
This is an old, old metaphor.
It has been June before.

Still the heart rises girlishly

this particular trip
to Safeway,

as the body sometimes
under familiar hands forgets
history, where the roads go, climbs
unwritten into sky and opens
petal after petal
of wild blue light.

Planned Parenthood
Claudia Van Gerven

It is 1947.
In a week I will break out of the ice floe of January.
I will be a red cry in a white world. I will flop
onto the belly of a woman who thinks I am
the last treasure she will fish up from these briny seas.

Father will mourn beneath his bright face, last chance
for a grown man to coo above tiny expanse
of blue veined chest, to grin like the lucky fisherman
with slippery, smelly freshness wiggling
in his hands.

But what are plans against the wish
to love perfectly?

We knew even then, swaddled in memory of Black
Tuesday, cribbed against our belief in the ration
book, my brother would come with his treasure of infant
curls, my sister would teethe on sentimental rusks.

Our wishes would dangle like hooks
through the ice of never enough.
We would always be
greedy for springs.

207

208

Deadheading
Dianalee Velie

White lacy curtains covered narrow, pane-glass panels, the windows in my grandparents' Brooklyn apartment. Three years old then...now I remember this: A shy, blonde toddler leaning my head against Aunt Pinky's large stomach, feeling my soon-to-be-born cousin, her first child, kicking inside her. Aunt Pinky expected this baby to arrive any day. I expected my Grandpa to come home.

Aunt Pinky pulled the curtains aside and we watched the big gray car, a car I now call a hearse, drive slowly past my grandparents' home, a walk-up railroad flat in Greenpoint, Brooklyn. Aunt Pinky cried, "Papa, Papa," her tears dripping down on to my curls, then cascading down my face. Licking my lips, I tasted salt. The sobbing rains conspired with my aunt, flailing against the windowpanes, bathing me in an emotion I would learn to call sorrow.

My first experience with death, with losing a man I loved, still plagues me when it rains, haunting me with darker interior clouds. Gray skies unearth my loneliness and fear. If my grandfather wasn't coming home anymore, as my aunt kept explaining between sobs, who would take me to Prospect Park? Who would peel the skin off the hot dogs the way he did for me? Who would let me sit outside on the fire escape taking the dead leaves off his prized geraniums? He told me you had to do that. You had to take the dead leaves and flowers off for new ones to grow. Deadheading it was called. I remember that.

At three years old, considered too young to go to the funeral, and with Aunt Pinky too pregnant, I bonded with her in grief. My cousin would be born the next day. My three-year-old brain wondered why Grandpa had to die for Ronnie, Aunt Pinky's son, to be born. But wasn't that what Grandpa had taught me? Just like his geranium plants, I reasoned, replenishing themselves after we deadheaded each one. Without ever attending the funeral, I learned death was permanent. Grandpa was gone, compost like fallen geranium leaves. Ronnie was here, a new bud, anxious to find light and bloom.

So Papa never came home, but I had a brand new cousin, the following year a brand new sister, the void left by Papa's death filling continuously with new life. Deadheading on the fire escape etched itself into my consciousness, growing like ivy, rooting on all the smooth surfaces of my young mind.

Because I was constantly hospitalized over the next few years for kidney infections, my fear of separation escalated. Mom busied herself at home with baby sister number two. My father, always the parent delivering me to the cold care of smiling nurses and doctors, eventually had to leave me behind those green antiseptic walls. Even with all Daddy's assurances that he would come back, every time he left me, I shook with terror. Would he ever return? I imagined, like Papa, he would vanish and the hearse carrying his coffin would drive past our New Jersey home. Who would be there to carry me on top of his shoulders? Who would teach me to swim? Who would always love me unconditionally and buy me butter pecan ice cream cones when I was sad?

Before Daddy left the hospital each night, he tenderly brushed my hair. Who would do that? I knew when he was finished brushing my hair, it would be time for him to leave. Hysteria came next. My time of horror. Time for me to carry on a tantrum, screaming for Daddy to come back. Please come back! I still smell the anesthesia, the ether, as I write these words. That scary mask, filled with an awful smell, lulled me to sleep, descending over and over again into the bitter taste of terror.

Memory of abandonment continued to appear, a phantom in my life, in my work. I continued to push it back into the deep belly of my brain. Through the years, persistently, it kept stealthily arriving, an unwanted visitor clothed in darkness, bearing poisoned fruitless fears. The older I became, the more I chose not to taste my Aunt Pinky's tears; the more I chose not to feel my unborn cousin's rage, begging for life, kicking against my Aunt's belly, kicking against my three-year-old sensibility, deeply pounding in the memory, making sure I would never forget.

I'm sure Papa meant to keep his promises. He wanted to take me to the park every Sunday. Daddy meant to keep his promises, too. Daddy said he would always be there for me. But one day he wasn't. Frozen in horror, I witnessed frightening red strobe lights, belonging to an ambulance in front of my house. Why? My lips dried. I tasted salt and pounding began in my brain. Racing up the stairs to my parent's home, I saw a body covered with a white sheet.

"Daddy, Daddy," I screamed. My mother's face was stoic. My cousin's feet kicked the side of my head. My Aunt Pinky's tears mixed with my own. Once again, the rain beat against the windowpane in Brooklyn, even though I was in New Jersey and almost a young woman. Another man I loved was never coming back. Gone.

I despised my three-year-old memory, engraved on the smoky mirror of my mind, clouding every decision and thought. I started to live life on the edge. I left home, hot with the fever of fear. I eloped with my childhood sweetheart. I raced death. I defied it. I drove dragsters and jumped horses. Anything to shake off that memory. I would not lose *this* man I loved. Death would not take him from me. It could have me first. But the memory, like a prowler, came creeping in the back window whenever I did not carefully lock all the doors to my psyche. I panicked if my husband was five minutes late. I would pull my own lace curtains aside every minute to see if the noise I just heard was his car turning into our driveway. If he had indigestion, I felt ill. The memory, like a stalker, was always there, even if, momentarily, it could not be seen. And then the prowler struck. It happened. I loved the third man to death. The third cherished heart stopped. Stopped in its prime, just when he was beginning to live. This sudden intrusive thief, this haunting memory was real.

"God, no! Joe! Joe!" I screamed to God. I screamed at God. I fell numb before God. Who would raise my children with me? Who would hold me in their arms every night? Who would share all my fears? Who would brush my hair when I was terrified? God had ignored my prayers. I wanted to die first. And then I just wanted to die.

I chastised myself. I would never stand in front of that Brooklyn window again. I would exile that memory forever. The memory, I believed, was the cause of all my sorrow. Somehow by holding on to that memory, the death of every man I ever loved became a reality. I hated my past. I would run again. I would quickly remarry. Anyone. I would not look back. But by not looking back, I stopped going forward. I stopped dreaming, awakening instead, frightened and in tears.

But then, during one especially bad nightmare, I forced myself to look out that Brooklyn window. I saw my three-year-old reflection engraved in tear-stained glass. I traveled back to the fire escape to comfort that terrified little girl, to finally hug her to my breast. With this love, she grew into a woman. Collecting all the lost memories of geraniums and fire escapes, sunshine and swimming, horses and cars, and first loves, I awoke. Memory had finally become my friend.

Now, I push aside the lace curtains of time. I see my husband, my father and my grandfather full of vitality, loving me as I loved them.

In my memory, none of them will ever age; they died forever young. When that familiar, strangely suffocating memory surfaces, I recognize the smell of ether, the fear of abandonment. I realize I am no longer that little girl. I've pulled aside the curtains, dull with the grime of fear. The rain has stopped, the sun is shining and I've begun looking for rainbows. I've opened all the windows to let in the warmth of self-knowledge. I've memorized the lesson: Deadheading, in the garden and in life, brings spectacular blooms. I will always see the world from high atop my father's shoulders, from Papa's fire escape in Brooklyn and from the height of my husband's love. The gentle radiance of those loves outshines even their deaths. The stalker has been arrested; for the first time, I am a free woman. At this moment, I smell no ether, taste no terror, as my lover gently brushes my hair.

The Last Decoy
John Weagly

I was sitting at my desk, feet up on my blotter, chin on my chest, trying to catch a couple of winks. I don't know why I bothered. For the past few months I hadn't gotten even a kitten of a catnap.

Just as I was about to give up on slumber, the office door opened. In walked the most beautiful woman I had ever seen. Five foot five and a careful amount of well proportioned voluptuousness. Short brown hair that...well, hair, legs, eyes, lips: fill in as many gorgeous clichés as you like, they all fit. She was wearing an outfit you'd find on a hooker in the seventies and on an eighth grade girl today. Everything about her was staggering.

She walked over to my desk and placed a business envelope on the blotter, next to my feet. "He didn't bite," she said.

"You hit him with everything?"

"And then some."

She sat down on the secondhand black-vinyl couch I kept in the office in case I wanted to fail at a lie down nap instead of a sitting up one.

I took my feet off the desk. "Give me the quick version."

"I went to his door. Told him my car broke down. Cell couldn't get a signal. Could I use his phone? Batted my eyes, wiggled my ass. He was a gentleman."

"Nothing."

"With a capital N."

Christine was my sex decoy. That's what I call it. The politically correct term, if there can be a politically correct term for something like this, is cheating decoy. When a woman thinks her man is untrustworthy, she comes to me. These clients don't think their significant others are cheating; they just think they might if the opportunity presented itself.

It's a dirty, distrustful world. I didn't make it that way; I just make a buck off the results.

I send Christine out and she tries to hook up with the potentially unfaithful. She flirts and winks but that's as far as she'll take it. Some guys go for her; some don't. This latest one didn't.

"So that's it," I said.

"That's it."

We looked at each other over my desk. There was a pain in my chest. This was her last assignment for me. She thought "Sex Decoy" wasn't a proper job for a married woman.

I drummed my fingers lightly on the blotter. It used to be green, now it was grey. My fingers made a faint hollow sound. "Listen," I said, "are you sure you..."

"Don't say it," she said.

"Don't say what?"

"I don't know, but whatever it is, I know you've said it before I know I don't want to hear it."

I was glad she stopped me. I wasn't sure what I was going to say either. It might not have been good.

We'd had a thing together back in high school. She'd been my first. You don't feel that way about too many people. At least I don't. After graduation, we broke up. I don't remember the reason why. Since then, we'd both stayed in Currie Valley, stayed friends, closer than friends, really. She worked full time as a teller at the Town & Country Bank & Trust, but she was always available when I needed her for one of my assignments.

Over the years we'd fallen into bed together here and there. On again, off again. Every time it happened, I thought we were getting back together, and every time she set me straight.

"It's just a thing, Barry," she'd say. "Something to get us through a dating dry spell. Don't get the wrong idea."

In my line of work it's sometimes hard to tell the difference between right and wrong.

On the night of the day Christine told me she was getting married, I had a dream that I was the one marrying her. We had a beautiful wedding, a beautiful relationship, a beautiful life. I was happier than I ever found myself in the real world. Waking up was like falling off of a cloud and crashing down to earth. I walked around depressed for the next three days, knowing I'd never recapture the elation I felt during that sleep.

I didn't want to ever feel like that again.

"There is one more thing," she said.

"What's that?"

She got up and walked over to the window. "We were wondering if you'd be an usher."

"What do you mean?"

"You know. At the ceremony. Ask people if they're friends of the groom or friends of the bride. Show them to their seats."

On the desk, my hands curled into fists. With the women I'd dated, it always felt like, in some way, I was cheating on Christine. Now here she was breaking my heart and I didn't even rate a spot in the real wedding party.

"What's the pay?" I asked.

She walked over and punched me in the shoulder. I could smell her perfume. It was the same stuff she wore our senior year. I wondered if her husband-to-be liked it as much as I did. "I need you there," she said. "You're my best friend. You can't be my maid of honor. This has to do."

I looked up at her. "Chris, are you sure?"

"I'm sure."

"I don't mean about me ushering."

"I know what you mean."

I could feel my fingernails digging into my palms. "I'll see you Saturday," I said.

"And you're okay with it?"

"I'll be there," I said.

After she walked out the door, I started to lower my head so I could make another try at a nap. Then I reminded myself.

I didn't want to ever have that dream again.

216

Love Sometimes Needs the Help of Thin, Pale Blue Envelopes

Anthony Russell White

When your need is the greatest
go to the hall closet and reach
past the tennis racquets and open
that box behind the old sweaters.
Take out the creased and faded
envelope with the quaint old stamps.
Press it to your cheek
and try to remember the scent
that was there.

218

The Luncheon
Marianne Wolf

would have married you," I whispered across the table, "but you never asked."

The fork he'd filled with a bit of cake and vanilla icing dropped away from his mouth and landed with a clink against his plate. Joe's face, warmed with a hint of blush from the merlot, turned ashen. He looked at me through his amber wire frames as if his eyes were really seeing me for the first time.

I jumped up. "I think I better find the powder room." As the chair jerked back, the dangle from my earrings rocked mid-air. Small stones of topaz, set in octagons of gold, I imagined they'd winked at Joe. It felt as though my body swayed right along with them. Wordless, Joe's forehead twisted like a child's Playdoh. Here it was, and I'd gone and made a fool of myself at 3 PM on a Thursday afternoon seated across from Joe in McCormick and Schmick's, on his 47th birthday, of all days.

I smiled then slipped out from the private snug, which kept our luncheon table tucked away from the view of the other diners. I bolted across the dark green carpeting, passed the glowing Tiffany-style lamps and framed prints depicting Chicago history, and at the end of a long calm hall, opened a mahogany door. Alone there, I wondered at the image staring back at me from the bathroom mirror: *Why in the world did you say that? What exactly did you expect him to do?*

How, I nodded as I slowly brushed my shoulder-length hair, *had I let it come to this?* I would have said yes. Even if I'd never really come out and told him so, I would have married him. I'd wanted an answer from Joe. For as long as I could remember, I'd wanted to hear him tell me he loved me – and always had. I just needed some reassurance; needed to hear him say that this business of being friends was nice, but wasn't enough for him. That's all it would have taken, though I was afraid to admit it.

I'd come a long way from the naïve coed I'd been my freshman year. I hadn't been prepared for that dark-haired boy with light and heat in his eyes. We'd met at the counter of the college commissary with dinner trays in our hands. In line, as I looked over the entrées, he stood staring through tinted wire-rims. With wavy hair and sideburns that could rival those of Elvis, he stood in bold plaid flannel shirt and worn bell-bottoms. I felt him long before he muttered "Hello." That Midwestern college student wasn't the impetuous, self-assured middle-aged woman who'd just revealed herself to this long-married man.

As I fumbled in my handbag for a lipstick, I pouted with pursed lips toward the mirror. *So what are you going to say now?* Pulling off its cap, I twisted the black Chanel tube and pressed the soft red crème against my lower lip and curved it into a grin, I remembered myself on that first date with Joe; a young woman in a paisley gauze blouse paired with tight hip huggers that dusted her platform sandals. My dark loose waves had framed my oval face and accented the green eyes now staring back at me. *I better get back out there before he thinks I've gone and done something else brash.* With a hard swallow I frowned, "Now sit at that table, smile and forget about it. What's done is done!"

I slid back into my chair just as Tony, our young waiter who resembled David Letterman, came to check on our table. "Anything else?" He smiled. The sound of poured ice dominated the table as he topped off our water glasses. Joe looked first towards the white-aproned young man, then with a purposeful gesture back to me.

"Whatever the pretty lady would like."

"I don't think I could eat another bite." I flushed, handing Tony my credit card. "This is my treat – it's your birthday. Remember, this luncheon is part of my gift to you."

"Well, thanks," he said. All angles in his tailored double-breasted suit, he'd arranged his equally angular features into a poker face, but melted into a gentle smile as he sat across from me. Joe folded the torn wrapping paper and fingered the boxed bottle of Calvados.

"You really don't have to; the present was already surprise enough. I didn't expect you..."

"Oh, but I do," I interrupted. "It's only fair."

Joe watched as I added a tip to the bill, signed the small slip of white paper and slid it into the leather folder. Tapping my fingertips against its embossed edge, I noticed the table lamplight reflected like stained glass against the baguettes in my wedding band. I thought how strange it was to be ending his birthday celebration this way, and hesitated before pushing the case towards the center of the cleared tablecloth. I'd said too much, and he'd said too little.

We rose from the table. Joe reached behind me, I thought to help with my coat. Instead he let it drop against my empty chair as he slipped his arms around my waist. I tilted my head up, confused. He moved a step closer and lowered his lips against mine. He let his lips

220

linger a moment before I could catch my breath, then pressed me hard against his chest and melted his mouth into mine. As his tongue slid between my lips I cupped my hands at the base of his head and clung to his taste. In all the years we'd known each other, amid all the gentle touches, we'd never kissed each other like this. And finally we both knew what each had hidden for half a lifetime.

Stunned, slowly I spoke, my lips not more than a few inches from his; "You've never kissed me like this before."

"No?" he whispered against the warmth of our breath. His skin brushed the edge of my lip and he pulled me closer, not wanting to release me just yet.

"This," I nodded light-headed in his arms, "I would have remembered." I let the fingertips of my right hand lightly feather through the thin salt and pepper hair at his temple. Normally so contained and controlled, it was the first time in 28 years that he'd seemed so vulnerable to me.

Wrapped in one another's arms and obscured from anyone's attention, we stood wordless in another fervent kiss. Stepping back I noted the intense look across Joe's face. I recognized that expression with a distinct sense of *déjà vu*. A smudge of my lipstick marked his lips. I smiled.

"Thank you," he said.

In all the years he'd been inviting me to dine with him, our luncheons had always lasted for hours. Never once had either of us rushed through a meal. We'd carved out time from busy schedules to catch up. On more than one occasion we'd lingered, listening to one another's stories. Over drops ringed at the bottom of our wine glasses, we'd hang onto what the other wanted to share during these meandering blocks of time. Never during these shared meals had either of us dared to admit what the other hoped; that good as a pair of friends, we may have been even better as lovers.

Joe pushed the revolving door. As we stepped out onto the sidewalk the assault from the frigid east wind shook me out of the moment. Numb, I stood watching him hail us a cab for the ride into the Loop. We sat shivering side by side as our breath swelled against the icy December afternoon. The sheer stocking, taut around my right calf, accidentally pressed against the gray glen-plaid of his tailored pant leg. I imagined I could feel the warmth of his body, though I knew that was impossible. It was the heat of my own body I felt growing beneath the multi-layers of fabric that came between us. Joe was holding his thick fur hat in his lap. As the cab moved, the hat's fur shimmered in the light: the vivid impression triggered the likeness of a buck suddenly caught in headlights.

"What a beautiful hat," I commented, "I've never seen anything like it in Chicago."

"You wouldn't. I bought it on a trip to Eastern Europe," he remarked twisting closer. "It comes in mighty handy on a day like today when I'm walking from the train." He placed a gloved hand over mine and squeezed it. "The wind's cold here, but it doesn't compare to the bitter winters there."

I had thought about that trip and his adoptive children. I closed my eyes as I thought of my own child I'd lost at the time he'd been making plans for his. Missed signals and failed opportunities had pulled us apart. He'd never asked me to marry him. All he'd done was make that silly bet during my last year on campus – a dozen long stemmed, white roses that I'd be engaged by graduation. Then he'd disappeared. And I waited. That June, the roses arrived. And I waited again. Before I knew it, six months had passed until that one afternoon when he'd sauntered into work. How did he know where I worked? Furious at the sight of him finally standing there, I'd sent him away, saying I had things to do. Then I heard he'd married someone else. Who'd told me? How was it that we'd started going out to lunch? It had been so long now, but we were each other's staunchest cheerleader.

222

The driver turned on the car radio and the WNUA jingle pricked the frigid air, followed by a jazz melody. With a quick bolt our shoulders lurched together and back against the vinyl seat patched by black electrical tape as our driver darted the yellow cab through the crowded traffic. The Chicago sky was now veiled in dusk above snowy city streets. The cab clipped along State Street, passing shadowed brownstones and frosted high-rises, their balconies littered with frozen terracotta pots and flowers frostbitten in the deadly kiss of the lake wind. I thought about how many women had been kissed on this street in the neighborhood's history. How many kisses, if any, had been as revealing as mine? Would a few hours of conversation and a pair of well-executed kisses transform two lives? Or would they complete them? Glancing past his shoulder, I could see the annual festival of flickering white lights appear to dance, swaying in the branches from the maples that line the pavement. Our late afternoon sky quickly faded into twilight against this canvas of miniature stars.

He tucked his arm under mine and we threaded our gloved fingers together as we rode through the Gold Coast area. Spellbound in silence, except for the cab's heater blowing hot air at a fevered pitch, we passed through residential blocks. The car drove past uniformed doormen draped in heavy formal coats hailing other cabs for their well-heeled tenants; purring limousines with tinted windows gliding towards waiting hotel lobbies; parishioners hurriedly scuffing their boot heels climbing toward Holy Name Cathedral as a hooded parish handyman salted the church steps.

At the corner of State and Grand our cab rolled to a stop as the traffic light turned red. Through the road-salted windows, I noticed a rag-tattered man standing there hawking *Streetwise* to no one in particular. Looking at him, I wondered – had there been some girl he'd loved?

A blue Volkswagen Jetta with a trio of college-aged coeds turned left in front of us, slowing in search of an open parking meter. Catching a glance from the raven-haired one, I imagined myself at her age. Surely, she must by now know her own young jean-clad, tongue-tied boy. Looking her in the eye, I wanted to roll down the window and shout to her, "Kiss him now! Let him kiss you now!" but instead I turned to focus back on my middle-aged man and smiled. Joe had been silent for much of the cab ride, as if he were thinking about the words rattling around in his head. I waited for him to say something.

Afternoon CTA buses wove in and out of designated bus lanes, picking up waiting curbside passengers, some with nylon backpacks flung over their shoulders, others with briefcases, and still others carrying green shopping bags from Marshall Field's. The cab chugged along in rhythm with the mounting traffic that paraded across the steel girders arched over the slapping water of the Chicago River. Behind them came the roar of a fire truck's heavy wheels racing over pavement, the siren's screaming pitch wailing above the water with the wind's whip. Caught up in the moment, I felt as though the entire city knew what I was feeling inside my body.

"Shall we drop you off first?" I gave his hand a squeeze as I motioned to the driver, "Two stops, cabbie – first one's at LaSalle and Washington."

Joe leaned into me as close as he could get and pulled off my gloves. I raised my hands to stroke his cheeks. His skin was still cold as I gently cupped my warm palms against his face. His smile widened. How many times had I pictured this smile and wondered why not me?

As we looked at each other, I almost giggled as if I were the coed he'd first met 28 years ago. Then, in a moment seemingly as long as those years, our lips touched fleetingly.

The cab pulled to a slow stop and Joe flung open the door. He twisted out and stood on the curb. I looked at him there, briefcase in hand, his birthday gift in the crook of his camel-haired arm. I sat pensive for a moment, then pulled the heavy door shut.

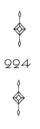

224

About the Contributors

● Bret Angelos, an attorney for the Illinois Department of Children and Family Services, earned degrees from the University of Chicago and Chicago-Kent College of Law. He has been writing short stories in the Bucktown Writer's Workshop since 2004.

● Donald Everett Axinn has written seven books of poetry and two novels including *Spin*, now a full-length feature film. He was awarded the Tennessee Williams Fellowship at Bread Loaf, and has been widely published in poetry journals

● Anastasia Bamford of Minnesota supports her writing habit with employment as a Veterinary Technician, and has two chapbooks: *Rejoice* and *Dogwood Girl.*

● Harker Brautighan keeps two pampered cats in Northern California, where she writes, lives and is an advocate for injured workers. Her work has appeared in national literary publications.

● Ute Carson emigrated to America from Germany in the 1960s. This Texas resident published her first short story in the 1970s and her first novel, *Colt Tailing,* in 2004.

● Michigan's Patricia Clark, author of *My Father on a Bicycle* and *North of Wondering*, is Professor in the Writing Department and Poet-in-Residence at Grand Valley State University and co-editor of an anthology called *Worlds in Our Words.* Clark is the winner of the 2004 Gwendolyn Brooks Poetry Award.

●Jim Curtiss writes, lives and teaches in Germany, where he explores intercultural and interlingual connections.

● Joanne Dalbo of New York has appeared in several prior Outrider anthologies and works as director of a domestic violence shelter for battered women and their children. Joanne juggles her career with her love of writing, reading, running, and her love of the outdoors.

● Marcy Darin of Illinois, whose first published fiction appears here, has worked as a newspaper reporter, editor for a women's magazine, and staff writer for several non-profits. Her articles have appeared in *The New York Times, Chicago Tribune* and *Ms. Magazine.*

● Indiana's Catherine Denby earned a scholarship to Notre Dame in Creative Writing, and teaches English and Western Literature at the college level.

● Randall DeVallance of Pennsylvania has work in The New Yinzer anthology *Dirt, McSweeney's, Eyeshot,* and *Facsimilation.* His novel *Dive* (2004) was published by Exquisite Cadaver Press.

● Virginia's Sue Eisenfeld has been published in *The Washingtonian, Virginia Living, The Sun,* and *Blue Ridge Country.* She is an environmental communications consultant to federal agencies in DC.

• Robert Klein Engler, poet, playwright, and president of Newtown Writers, is no stranger to The Windy City's stages, where *Cayetano's Circus* debuted in 2005. He has won multiple Illinois Arts Council awards.

• Bertil Falk of Trelleborg, Sweden, a retired Swedish journalist and TV producer, spent over 10 years in international newsrooms, wrote 16 published books, and has short fiction in English in *Ellery Queen's Mystery Magazine* and *Alfred Hitchcock's Mystery Magazine*.

• Lynn Fitzgerald of Chicago has an M.A. in Creative Writing and Comparative Literature. She has received the Joanne Hirschfeld Award and three National Endowment for the Humanities awards. Her work appears in *After Hours, Word Salad, Kalliope, The English Journal* and other publications.

• Illinois' Maureen Tolman Flannery's *Ancestors in the Landscape: Poems of a Rancher's Daughter* has been nominated for a Pulitzer Prize. Her other books are *A Fine Line; Secret of the Rising Up: Remembered Into Life;* and *Knowing Stones.* Her work is in 40 anthologies and over 100 literary reviews including *Midwest Quarterly Review, Amherst Review, Slant, Bucklee*, and *Atlanta Review.*

• Pat Gallant of New York City has been published in *Saturday Evening Post, Writers Digest, Byline, Poet Magazine, Simple Pleasures of Friendship* and the nationally known *Chicken Soup...* series.

• Barbara Goldowsky of New York has published two books of poetry and a book of short stories. Her writings appear in *Byline, Caprice, Midwest Poetry Review, St. Andrews Review,* and *Perceptions.*

• Phil Gruis of Idaho, a former editor of daily newspapers, has work in *Plainsongs, Dirt, Main Channel Voices, Bear Deluxe, Poetry Motel, Erosha, Love's Chance* and *Pontoon.*

• Illinois' Mary Ann Grzych has had poetry published. This is her first published fiction.

• Carol Haggas of Chicago is a freelance writer with work in regional publications. A member of the National Book Critics Circle, she regularly reviews for *Booklist* and *ForeWord* magazines.

• New York City's Melanie Hammer teaches writing and has fiction and essays in literary magazines, including *The Ohio Review, The Nebraska Review, Under the Sun, Flyway,* and *The Missouri Review.*

• Susan Hannus of Illinois writes short fiction and poetry. Her work has been published in *Byline, Seeding the Snow,* and *Take Two, They're Small.*

• Juley Harvey of California is a prize-winning poet with work in dozens of literary publications including *Earth Beneath, Sky Beyond.*

• Nancy J. Heggem of Illinois, a Trustee of the Palatine Public Library District, is on the Board of the N. Suburban Library System. She has been published in the *Daily Herald* and *Family Gatherings.*

• Linda Heilscher of Illinois has poetry has featured in various anthologies, and she is presently working on a novel.

• Illinois' Herb Jackson, whose fiction has appeared in *Chicago Works: A New Collection of Chicago Authors Best Stories,* has received the Dwight C. Follett Fellowship for Fiction, the National Gold Circle's 1st Place Award for Traditional Fiction for Magazines and three Ragdale Fellowships.

• Grace Papelera Kavanaugh of Illinois announces this is her first published work.

• Marie Loggia-Kee of California is a freelance writer who teaches English at the University of Phoenix and National University.

• Austin Kelly lives and writes in Chicago, where he performs his work at Open Mics. He has work in *Take Two* and *Family Gatherings.*

• K.B. Laugheed of Indiana gardens, tends her animals, and is at work on a novel.

• Connecticut attorney Harmon Leete's publications include two contest awards and appearances in a previous "Black-and-White" anthology.

• Virginia's Lyn Lifshin, a legend in small press publishing circles, has published over 100 books of poetry, and is the subject of an award-winning documentary film, *Lyn Lifshin: Not Made of Glass.* Recent prizewinning titles include *Before It's Light.*

• Ellaraine Lockie of California has published three nonfiction books, plus numerous magazine articles/columns and children's stories. Nominated for seven Pushcart Prizes in poetry, she has four published chapbooks: *Midlife Muse, Crossing the Center Line, Coloring Outside the Lines,* and *Finishing Lines.*

• Paul Martin of Pennsylvania has poetry in *Commonweal, Green Mountain Review, New Letters, Nimrod, Passages North, Poetry East* and *Texas Poetry Review.* He has three chapbooks plus book-length work, *Closing Distances,* finalist in the May Swenson and Poetry House competitions.

• Prize-winning Illinois poet Frank Matagrano has a chapbook in the Pudding House Press "Greatest Hits" series – *Frank Matagrano's Greatest Hits, 1995-2005* – and a full-length poetry collection, *I Can Only Go as Fast as the Guy in Front of Me.*

• Ohio's Candice Mayes graduated Kent State University with a B.A. in English and a Writing minor. Her prize-winning poetry appears in publications including *English Journal.*

• Iowa's John McBride has poetry in over a dozen poetry journals. His work has won awards at the national level.

• Illinois' Kathy McElligott performs at Chicago's open mics and is at work on a novel. This is her first published poetry.

• Canada's Elaine Ruth Mitchell is a Toronto teacher and writer. This recent recipient of an Ontario Arts Council grant is a past winner in the "Black-and-White" competitions.

• Leana Page of Illinois, a retired telecommunications executive, has work in earlier Outrider Press "Black-and-White" anthologies. She has been a featured reader at venues including Printers Row Book Fair and Twilight Tales.

• Illinois' Natalie Pepa has an MFA in creative writing from Vermont College and has work appearing in *Latino Stuff Review, Poetry Motel, Rockhurst Review, Whetstone, Karamu,* and others.

• Wisconsin's Nancy Rafal is the Wisconsin Fellowship of Poets treasurer and has been published in *Hummingbird, Free Verse,* and past "Black-and-White" anthologies. She is one-third of the performance poetry group, The Off Q Gals. Their first chapbook is *Slightly Off Q.*

• Mike Robinson of California is a 21-year-old Illustration student and filmmaker whose first novel is *Vermin Street:Life in These Walls.*

• Kimberly Rosen is the pen name of a Maine physician, artist and writer whose past work appears in *Family Gatherings* and other Outrider Press publications.

• Dr. Lynn Veach Sadler of North Carolina is widely published, and has won *The Pittsburgh Quarterly's* Hay Prize; tied for first in *Kalliope's* Elkind Contest; and won the Poetry

Society of America's 2003 Hemley Award and *Asphodel's* 2003 Poetry Contest.

• Shawntelle Santas of New York has work in *At-Home Mother, The Writer, Woman's Day* and a variety of regional and specialty publications.

• Ron Savage of Virginia earned a BA and MA in psychology and a doctorate in counseling, all from the College of William and Mary, and has worked for over 25 years as a hospital psychologist. His stories have appeared in *Film Comment, Modern Short Stories, Tomorrow Magazine,* and *The Magazine of Fantasy and Science Fiction.*

• Illinois' Rev. Susan Baller-Shepard was part of the University of Iowa's undergraduate Writer's Workshop and has studied poetry at Illinois State University. Her essays and poetry have appeared in the *Chicago Tribune, Writer's Digest, the Peoria Journal Star,* and on-line sites for Woman Made Gallery and *Rhino* poetry magazine.

• Prize-winning poet Margie Skelly of Chicago teaches writing classes at Loyola University and has been published in numerous literary journals and anthologies.

• Grazina Smith of Chicago has been published previously in Outrider Press anthologies including *Take Two – They're Small* and *Family Gatherings* and in *Kaleidoscope Ink, Women's World, Chicken Soup for the Woman's Soul* and *The Sun* magazine. She has won national fiction writing awards.

• Washington DC's Mary L. Tabor has a collection of short stories, *The Woman Who Never Cooked*, winner of the Mid-List Press's First Series Award. Her fiction has recently appeared in *Image, the Mid-American Review, Chelsea, Hayden's Ferry Review,* and *American Literary Review.*

• Keith Vanden Eynden of Ohio has published a dozen poems and a novel, *Let Us Divided Live.* His short story, "Making a Mark," won the 2001 City Beat/Mercantile Library Short Story Contest. He also has work in *Things That Go Bump in the Night.*

• For the past two years, Ohio's Rose Vanden Eynden's short stories have garnered second place prizes in Outrider Press' *Family Gatherings* and *Things That Go Bump in the Night* anthology competitions. She has also published short fiction in *The Circle* online. Her nonfiction manuscript is *So You Want to be a Medium? A Practical Guide to Working Between the Worlds.*

• Colorado's Claudia Van Gerven has poetry published in a number journals and anthologies. Her chapbook, *The Ends of Sunbonnet Sue,* won the 1997 Angel Fish Press Prize and her book, *The Spirit String,* was a finalist in several national contests, including the 2003 Bright Hill Poetry Contest.

• New Hampshire writer/teacher Dianalee Velie has a full-length poetry book, *Glass House.* This member of the National League of Pen Women and the International Women's Writing Guild has been internationally published in journals including *Kalliope, Potomac Review* and *The South Dakota Review.*

• John Weagly of Chicago won the 2004 Norumbega Fiction Award for Best Short Story Collection for *The Undertow of Small Town Dreams.* He has work in previous "Black-and-White" anthologies including *Family Gatherings* and *Things That Go Bump in the Night.*

• Prize-winning poet and self-described "pilgrim, poet and healer" Anthony Russell White lives on a California mountaintop and serves on the permanent staff of the Nine Gates Mystery School. His work appear in national publications.

• Marianne Wolf of Chicago, an MFA candidate in the Fiction Writing Program of Columbia College Chicago, has stories in the anthologies *Family Gatherings* and *Things That Go Bump,* both by Outrider Press. She is the 3rd place winner of the Illinois Woman's Press Associations, Mate E. Palmer 2004 Communications Award. Her writing also appears in *Zajednicar,* the national newspaper of the Croatian Fraternal Union of America.

About the Judge

Lee Martin is the author of two novels, *The Bright Forever*, (Shaye Areheart Books, 2005), and *Quakertown* (Dutton, 2001). He has also published two memoirs, *Turning Bones* (University of Nebraska Press, 2003), and *From Our House* (Dutton, 2000), which was a Barnes and Noble Discover Great New Writers selection and a nominee for the Pultizer Prize and the National Book Award. His story collection, *The Least You Need to Know* (Sarabande, 1996), was the winner of the Mary McCarthy Prize in Short Fiction. His stories and essays have appeared in such places as *Harper's*, *The Georgia Review*, *Creative Nonfiction*, *The Kenyon Review*, *The Southern Review*, *Story*, *DoubleTake*, *Glimmer Train*, *Shenandoah*, *Fourth Genre*, *River Teeth*, and *Prairie Schooner*.

He has won fellowships from the National Endowment for the Arts and the Ohio Arts Council as well as the Lawrence Foundation Award, The Jeanne Charpiot Goodheart Prize, and The Glenna Luschei Prize for Literary Distinction. A native of Illinois, he is now Professor of English in the creative writing program at The Ohio State University.

230

About TallGrass Writers Guild

TallGrass Writers Guild is open to all who write seriously at any level. The Guild supports members by providing performance and publication opportunities via its six-page, bi-monthly newsletter, open mikes, formal readings, annual anthologies, and the TallGrass Writers Guild Performance Ensemble programs.

In affiliation with Outrider Press, TallGrass produces its annual "Black-and-White" anthologies, the results of international calls for themed contest entries. Cash prizes and certificates awarded result from the decisions of independent judges.

The Guild is a rarity among arts organizations in that it neither seeks nor accepts federal funding because of the creative limitations imposed by such grants, often of an arbitrary and political nature. For more information on TallGrass Writers Guild membership and programs, call 708-672-6630 or toll-free at 1-800-933-4680 (code 03). Email tallgrasswriters@aol.com .

About the Editor

Whitney Scott plays many roles in Chicago's literary scene. She is an author, editor, book designer and reviewer whose poetry, fiction and creative nonfiction have been published internationally, earning her listings in *Contemporary Authors* and *Directory of American Poets and Fiction Writers*. Her work has appeared in respected reviews and journals, including *Howling Dog, Kaleidoscope Ink, Pearl, Potomac Review, Art & Understanding, Amethyst, CQ, The Poetry Peddler, Arts Alive, Dangerous Dames, The F.O.C. Review, Tomorrow Magazine, After Hours* and others. She was a 2004 Featured Poet online at *This Hard Wind.*

A member of the Society of Midland Authors, she performs her work at colleges, universities, arts festivals and literary venues throughout the Chicago area and has been featured as guest author in the Illinois Authors Series at Chicago's Harold Washington Library. Scott regularly reviews books for the American Library Association's *Booklist* magazine.

Whitney has studied with the U.S. Poet Laureate Ted Kooser; internationally acclaimed writer Grace Paley; New Mexico's state artist-in-residence, novelist Miriam Sagan; as well as with authors Carol Anshaw, Rita Mae Brown, Pulitzer Prize winner Robert Olen Butler, Richard Carter, Denise Chavez, Albert Goldbarth, Pulitzer Prize nominee Lee Martin and Elizabeth Tallent.

In addition to working one-on-one with developing writers, Whitney runs a variety of writers' workshops and has headlined the Taste of Chicago Writers conference. She has presented writing seminars at DePaul and Northwestern Universities and taught poetry workshops at the renowned Off-Campus Writers Workshop. Whitney teaches in the Professional Writing Program at Columbia College/Chicago.

Outrider Press Publications

___ **Falling in Love Again** – $17.95 _____
Writings on revisiting romance, beloved locales and more

___ **Things That Go Bump in the Night** – $17.95 _____
Writings on the supernatural from horrific to hilarious

___ **Family Gatherings** – $17.95 _____
Writings on families

___ **Take Two — They're Small** – $17.95 _____
Writings on food

___ **A Kiss Is Still A Kiss** – $16.95 _____
Writings on romantic love

___ **Earth Beneath, Sky Beyond** – $16.95 _____
An anthology on nature and our planet

___ **Feathers, Fins & Fur** – $15.95 _____
Writings on animals

___ **Freedom's Just Another Word** – $14.95 _____
Poetry, fiction and essay on freedom

___ **Alternatives: Roads Less Travelled** – $14.95 _____
Writings on counter-culture lifestyles

___ **Prairie Hearts** – $14.95 _____
Short fiction and poetry on the Heartland

___ **Dancing to the End of the Shining Bar** – $9.95 _____
A novel of love and courage

Illinois residents add 8½ % [.085] sales tax
Add shipping charges:
$3.95 for one book _____
$5.95 for two books _____
$1.75 for each additional book _____

Send Check/$ Order to:
Outrider Press, Inc.   **Total** ═══
937 Patricia
Crete, IL 60417   www.outriderpress.com
outriderpr@aol.com

232